Mrs. Caldwell
Speaks to Her Son

Mrs. Caldwell Speaks to Her Son

By CAMILO JOSÉ CELA

Mrs. Caldwell habla con su hijo

in the authorized English translation
and with an introduction by
J. S. BERNSTEIN

Cornell University Press

ITHACA AND LONDON

First published 1968
Second printing 1990
First printing, Cornell Paperbacks, 1968
Third printing 1991

International Standard Book Number 0-8014-0073-2 (cloth)
International Standard Book Number 0-8014-9783-3 (paper)

Library of Congress Catalog Card Number: 68-16379

PRINTED IN THE UNITED STATES OF AMERICA

Contents

vii

viii

xii

Cela's Mrs. Caldwell

Camilo José Cela was thirty-seven when *Mrs. Caldwell Speaks to Her Son* was first published in 1953. He had previously published four novels: *The Family of Pascual Duarte* (1942), *Rest Home* (1943), *New Adventures and Misadventures of Lazarillo de Tormes* (1944), and *The Hive* (1951). By the time of *Mrs. Caldwell's* appearance Cela was widely known in Spain and abroad, and was considered by many to be the *enfant terrible* of modern Spanish letters. Some critics charged him with inventing *tremendismo*, a sort of fiction obsessed with the sensational and scabrous, while others countered by observing that scenes as violent and characters as distasteful could be found throughout Spanish literature, from the *Celestina* and Quevedo down to modern times. Cela himself disavowed his putative paternity of *tremendismo* and refused to alter. He remained through the fifties an incontrovertible presence, founding in 1956 *Papeles de Son Armadans*, Spain's foremost literary magazine, which he continues to edit, and which has become for our day what Ortega y Gasset's *Revista de Occidente* was for his. In his nonfictional writings Cela has stressed the obligation of the writer to bear witness to his age. But the testimonial imperative does not lead to an objective realism, or a preconceived, hence biased, naturalism. Rather it results in the transformation of consensual reality by means of highly conscious style, advocacy of vitality and activity in all human relationships, and a good deal of black humor.

One is struck by the great restlessness and variety of Cela's fiction. His first five novels treat widely different themes and display several distinct prose styles. His more recent work, *Crowd of Loveless Fables* and *New Scenes of Madrid Life* for example, extends and deepens the range of his fiction, on the one hand re-creating stories from Greek myth, and on the other penetrating further, one might say microscopically, into a Madrid already uncovered in *The Hive*.

The testimonial imperative, as I have called it, has other outcomes as well. Not only the "realism" of urban Madrid, but the reality of Spanish life in the provinces, finds expression in his work, principally in his travel books. Cela is an indefatigable traveler, exploring the remote corners of Spain as some of the Generation of 1898, Azorín, Baroja, Unamuno, had done. But his purpose is not so much to discover and explain the roots of Spanish social and political malaise as to experience and testify to them. Tireless travel in Europe, South America, the United States, attests, it seems to me, to Cela's openness, his readiness to accept, even affirm, whatever life brings him.

In his receptivity to all of life Cela rejects the withdrawal of a Proust, the regionalism of a Blasco Ibáñez, and in this way takes the temper of his age. *Papeles* shows a marked receptivity in its timeliness and pertinence. However, certain factors mitigate against the complete expression of his testimony to life, and lead Cela to transform it, to evade some things which the reader knows underlie the testimony. One of these factors is an impulse to style which pervades all his writings; another has been perhaps the censorship of the Spanish press.

The evasiveness occasioned by political reality gives rise

to notable ambiguities in Cela. While he lives in Spain, he does not live in its cultural or political center, but on the margin, in Majorca. Though he is a member of the Royal Spanish Academy, he almost never attends its monthly meetings. His refusal to join his countrymen in exile elicits, on occasion, their rancorous criticism. Yet his insistence on living in Spain betrays at once a personal love of country—not by any means of the *patria chica*—as well as the necessity to bear witness, at first hand, for posterity.

Ambiguity and evasiveness mark his work, which is almost as much as to say that his work is poetic. In its fundamental assumptions, Cela's stance before the novel shows certain clear poetic techniques: the use of allusion rather than direct statement, abundant metaphor, the explanation of symbols in the work by their juxtaposition with already known elements. Yet his fictions are not *poèmes en prose* primarily, as were those of his compatriots Benjamín Jarnés and Rosa Chacel, for his paramount concern is not exclusively aesthetic.

Mrs. Caldwell is a strange book. Cela has called it "a novel poorly understood by others and one for which I have a special affection." [1] It strikes one as strange because there does not seem to be any way in, any entree, to the confusing reminiscences of the elderly Englishwoman. The reader may feel, at the end, that the diary is indeed nothing but the maunderings of a sick mind; Mrs. Caldwell does, after all, end in an asylum. The subjects upon which her attention is focused seem to have little connection one with another. They enter and leave her consciousness with a dizzying facility and speed. One may feel that the work is but a kaleidoscopic tour de force, meant to confound and amaze.

[1] Letter to the translator, dated at Palma de Mallorca, 10 January 1965.

But perhaps it is more than that. It seems, first of all, a poetic exposition of Mrs. Caldwell's intense love for her son.[2] Second, it is an apparently realistic vision of life among what we could call the *petite aristocratie*. Third, it is a commentary on certain kinds of mothering which, the truth be told, are as much Spanish as English. Beneath all the madness the hard ring of truth resounds in Mrs. Caldwell's confession of her love gone haywire.

What manner of novel is this then? Above all, it is a highly poetic treatment of an alienated mind. Anthony Kerrigan, translator of Cela's *The Family of Pascual Duarte*, has said that because of its poetry "it appears to be virtually untranslatable into a non-Romance language."[3] How odd that the depiction of this Englishwoman's emotional life should seem untranslatable into English. Were it true, we should have to grant that Mrs. Caldwell's verbal production was equivalent to a madwoman's ravings and had become hermetic and inaccessible. Yet, if her language is indeed poetic, highly individualized, the subject matter is universal. Mrs. Caldwell's Englishness is tinged with Spanish elements, a hint that what concerns her transcends national boundaries. We can begin to penetrate the work's obscurity by examining this novelistic mixing of national characteristics.

When Cela first met Mrs. Caldwell, he tells us, she was removing historic tiles from the Princess of Eboli's bedroom. Tiles are a favorite souvenir with which the tourist returns from his trip to Spain; but they are not ordinarily a souvenir of England. From the outset, then, there is something Spanish about the setting of the novel. In Chapter 12, Mrs. Cald-

[2] Paul Ilie (*La novelística de Camilo José Cela* [Madrid, 1963], p. 165) makes a similar observation.

[3] "Camilo José Cela and Contemporary Spanish Literature." *Western Review*, XXII (1958), 296.

well mentions how lucky they were to find some good Scotch in time for the party. Scotch, and good quality Scotch, has not been particularly hard to find in England, but it has been at times rather rare and expensive in Spain. In Chapter 6, Mrs. Caldwell betrays traces of Spanishness when she speaks of the American who was "escorted to the border." Obviously, the English do not deport people this way; but the Spanish do. Again, Mrs. Caldwell recalls Louise MacDucaud Tomlinson by her maiden, not her married, name, a practice more common to the Spanish than to the English. For a Spanish woman does not lose her maiden name on marrying. She adds her husband's family name to her own; but among her friends the woman is still referred to as Louise MacDucaud, not as Louise Tomlinson. Beneath Mrs. Caldwell's Englishness there is a Spanish substrate which has its effect on her thinking. When we recall that Cela's mother was English, the fusion of the two nationalities does not seem quite so surprising.

We observe that Mrs. Caldwell is part of an old order now in decline. Her husband had his club, as proper English gentlemen do (Chap. 28). She disparages work (Chap. 33). The family was used to summers away from the city (Chap. 70). Mrs. Caldwell is frequently concerned with ancestors, legacies, and inheritances. This often (as in Chapter 70) has a more specific connotation than the general economic one; often she is at pains to discover why her son's lot was to die young, why this was the legacy left to him. Her opinions of many things, for example boardinghouses, teaching orphans how to fence, colored people, second-class funerals, having cherimoyas with kümmel, are those of an aristocrat come down in the world.

This descent, with its attendant economic distress, involves a moral decline as well. For Mrs. Caldwell has had amorous affairs with a number of men other than her husband: the man from the second floor, Sebastian Rico, Carlo Dominici, the caseless lawyer, Tom Dickinson, an Italian marquis, and the chum with the permanent smile. In fact, her son is not the son of her husband, to whom she usually refers with a pious "God rest his soul," but of the man from the second floor (Chaps. 2 and 41), "who was always so helpful."

Mrs. Caldwell's polyandry is a direct comment on the morals of an aristocracy in decline. The patterns of good breeding, both in the sense of proper bloodlines and of good manners, which so occupy her thoughts, have broken down. Her son is illegitimate, and has bad manners (e.g., he picks his nose [Chap. 1]). Furthermore, her many lovers bespeak an attempt on her part to get back at Eliacim for his interest in the opposite sex. If Eliacim can be linked, even if only in her phantasy, with Miss Stadford, Miriam the lyrist, her friend Rosa, and Dorothy, then she may feel justified in her own affairs with many men. Also indicative of this decline are the ways in which her love is satisfied with others—for example, her being whipped by the Italian marquis.

Mrs. Caldwell's love for Eliacim is of course strongly incestuous (Chap. 204). In this respect, we have a reversal of the story of *The Family of Pascual Duarte*. In Cela's first novel, the incestuous feelings of a brutal and violent peasant toward his mother, herself an ignorant and repellent woman, cause him to stab her to death. Now we have a shift in social class, tone, and point of view. Mrs. Caldwell and Eliacim seem refined and sensitive, she loves rather than hates her son. We see their relations exclusively from her viewpoint. Since Eliacim died before the book begins, his mother's feelings cannot result in any action toward or against him. Instead, their relationship in the novel is endowed by her phantasy with a vague and insubstantial quality.

Part of Cela's great originality lies precisely here, for very seldom in literature has a work been given over entirely to the portrayal of the viewpoint of the mother in an incestuous mother-son relationship. One notable presentation of such a viewpoint can be found, however, in *Letters from Jenny*, a volume of actual letters, expressive and literary, that presents a similar picture of a mother's frustrated love for her son.[4] Here also the son has died prematurely, and the woman ends in an institution. Jenny's letters are sent to a young couple, contemporaries of her son, who support her and correspond with her. The same constellation of personality traits may be found in Jenny as in Mrs. Caldwell: alienation and feelings of having been abandoned, self-pity, pessimism, distrust of others, and guilt. Jenny feels betrayed by her son, as does Mrs. Caldwell. The underlying reason is that the son has failed to return her love.

One important concomitant of the intimacy between Mrs. Caldwell and Eliacim which makes its impact in the original but is impossible to render adequately in English is that she addresses him throughout with the second-person-singular pronoun, "tú," the English "thou." [5] Eliacim uses the same form with his mother. As in French, German, and other languages, the use of the intimate form of address responds to certain assumptions in the culture which are universally, but not always consciously, accepted.[6] In the novel, as generally, the reciprocal use of "tú" indicates reciprocity of feelings

[4] Edited and interpreted by Gordon Allport (New York, 1965). This book is an expansion of an earlier article by Allport, under the same title, which appeared in the *Journal of Abnormal and Social Psychology*, XLI (1946), 315–350 and 449–480.

[5] Cela has written (in the preface to the second Spanish edition [Barcelona, 1958]), that *Mrs. Caldwell* was an attempt to carry the use of the second-person-singular pronoun as far as he could without confusing the reader.

[6] Cf. Roger Brown, *Social Psychology* (New York, 1965), pp. 51–100, and especially pp. 54–71, where Brown discusses "The Historical Evolution of the European Pronouns of Address."

and solidarity. However, we should bear in mind that the novel purports to be autobiographical; hence, everything in it is seen from Mrs. Caldwell's vantage point and Eliacim is quoted directly on only a very few occasions, principally in the early chapters. That is, Mrs. Caldwell is the only authority for Eliacim's use of the intimate pronoun with her; the reader is given no other source in the novel to report on his usage of the pronoun. Therefore, he is made to use the intimate form of address partly in order to foster the impression that he reciprocates her feelings.

The active fictional presence of the son fades as the work progresses; he has a measure of fictional independence only when he is directly quoted in the early portion. As Eliacim fades as an active presence speaking and reacting in his own right, rather than through the descriptions of his mother, he is correspondingly seen more and more through her phantasies, until he recedes entirely toward the end. The recession of Eliacim in the increasingly self-centered phantasies of his mother marks her progressive alienation which, as we have noted, ends in her insanity.

Setting the book as an autobiographical account of a mother's incestuous feelings for her son posed two distinct problems for Cela: psychological accuracy in depiction, and justification for Mrs. Caldwell's statements. What she feels must somehow take a shape other than the transparently Freudian, if it is to succeed as artistic prose. Assuming her incestuous love, the problem is how to transform it, disguise it as it were, to reduce its blatant sexuality, the shocking possessiveness Mrs. Caldwell feels toward Eliacim. Herein lies, for example, one reason for the tremendous emphasis Mrs. Caldwell gives to the changing shapes of things, and to the process of transformation in general; for the same reason she praises adaptability and inconstancy (Chap. 172). Her phantasy is constantly in a state of *becoming*, conjuring the possible in the unlikely. This is a poetic symbolization of the central problem at issue: how can she *change* from Eliacim's mother into his lover?

Let us recall some of these changes: she imagines herself changed into a handful of dung, or into a spider; Eliacim's skull becomes a bedroom for jellyfish; the devil changes shape, becoming a dog, a spider, a tremor on the wall; she imagines God changing her into a cactus leaf; children fear turning into statues of salt; she wishes to become a sea siren, a sea breeze, sea sand. We could add other examples to this list of phantasy transformations. And we could justifiably include a great many transformations which are more properly called metaphors, for example, her son in his figured pajamas would look like a bird of paradise. All the changes, abrupt, outlandish, even morbid, represent her way of evading her essential nature as the mother of her beloved. Against the inevitability of her condition her phantasy life irrepressibly unleashes a host of potentialities. If these potentialities occurred in the mind of a normal, sane person, we might speak of him as caught up in the existential dilemma of choosing. The possibilities here are not real, however, and the only change which would be satisfying for Mrs. Caldwell, Eliacim's rebirth, is impossible.

The second major problem is that of the first-person narrative. The book is a diary, a relation of what Mrs. Caldwell did, what she said, what she thought. We have only her word for the events narrated. No Apollonian novelist controls the work, manipulating and revealing other characters' inmost thoughts and feelings so as to corroborate or contrast with her account. Hence the reader may inquire how aware she is of what she reveals about herself. At some points she seems fairly obtuse, that is, unaware of the inner meanings her phantasies convey. When she and Eliacim go fishing, the experience seems to have an air of innocence which hides from Mrs. Caldwell its very romantic implications (Chap. 24). At other times, however, she sheds the obtuse stance and indicates clearly that she fully understands the implications of her phantasies (Chaps. 4 and 204).

Though she may in fact be aware of the general implication of her phantasies, Mrs. Caldwell seems not to recognize many of their particular manifestations. For example, she tells us that the maternal instinct arose in her the day her son wore long pants for the first time (Chap. 98). Obviously, since *her* maternal instinct is equated with sexual love, she first loves Eliacim on the day he becomes a man, that is, capable of returning her love. Her love for him leads to jealousy of other women in his life (Chaps. 96 and 160). When she conjures up girl friends or possible spouses for him, they are flawed—Miss Stadford is consumptive, Dorothy dies in hospital—or grotesquely mutilated—Miriam the lyrist. Her phantasies serve to placate her jealousy, removing or deforming the women who might be eligible mates for her son.

The grotesque humor characteristic of Cela emerges from a further, more destructive, stage of her phantasy life. For she hints strongly at her son's effeminacy: he resembles a ladies' hairdresser (Chap. 12), he waves at the girls waiting for their boy friends but has no girl friend himself (Chap. 18), he resembles a young girl (Chap. 174). Endowing Eliacim with effeminate traits safely removes the danger that he will, even in her phantasy, turn his affections toward a woman other than herself. But beyond that it is a kind of inner censorship which serves to restrain her amorous impulse. As if in her phantasy she feared the consummation of her love, she tends to perceive Eliacim as effeminate in order to remove from him the capacity for satisfying her love. The same perception informs the innocence with which she recounts some of their experiences, for example, the trip about the bed (Chap. 38). The grotesque element appears as a function of her almost constant predilection for the flawed and broken, the diseased and unfortunate. She patronizes a caseless lawyer and an incompetent tailor. The novel is permeated with decay and death.

Characteristically, again, Cela does not paint an entirely pessimistic picture, for her phantasies themselves are an indisputable sign of creativity and vitality. And in a manner we could call Cervantine or Galdosian, he endows Mrs. Caldwell with a *pícara idea*, an informing folly, which propels her, as it had Don Quixote and Fortunata, through the book. Mrs. Caldwell's overriding folly is her refusal to accept Eliacim's death—hence the great thematic importance of hope in her phantasies. The manner of his death, drowning in a distant sea, almost permits her to hope that somehow he may have escaped death and may return. Thus, her refusal to accept his death makes her endow him with various shapes in death (Chap. 50), prolonging his existence in her phantasy. In fact we could say that Mrs. Caldwell *vive desviviéndose*, she lives a sort of hope in despair.

The language of *Mrs. Caldwell* is quite precise. Her diary is full of specific concrete names of things, for example, the four stomachs of ruminants. She says that everything needs its own name (Chap. 40). This propensity for naming has obsessive overtones which are also reflected in the many collections of things mentioned in the novel. She wishes she had a collection of wild flowers; Uncle Albert had a river collection. The very titles of Chapters 56 and 103 show this obsessiveness. Collecting things and cataloguing them require precision, enthusiasm, and perseverance, all of which characterize her love for her son. Almost as a foil for the impression of vagueness in which she would envelop her love, her language betrays its concreteness. Her love is specifically that and nothing less. The properly furnished wax museum, the well-equipped operating room, the inventory she mentions at the end, are all complete. Likewise, there are no loose ends in the novel. Her love exists as an integral, perfect whole. The precision of language lends a powerful impression of realism to the narration which is juxtaposed with the very unreal phantasy life which makes up the narration's content. The obsessiveness reaches its culmination in Chapter 178, "The Iceberg," where, with unparalleled stylistic inventiveness, Cela writes out all the syntactic permutations of a four-phrase sentence.

Another mark of Mrs. Caldwell's obsessiveness is seen in her repetitions. Each chapter is full of the repetition of epithets and phrases, and of chapter titles. Of course, as we noted above, the entire novel is an exploration of one theme from many perspectives. No matter what specific object occupies her attention, no matter how precise or recondite its nature, it always leads Mrs. Caldwell repetitively to the same fact: her love for Eliacim.

The novel's many short, episodic chapters are actually complete poetic images; although some of the same images recur, there is little overlap from chapter to chapter. This is a novel, then, without a strict narrative line or conventional plot. Rather it is a poetic portrait of Mrs. Caldwell's phantasies and love, made up of 213 distinct but related brush strokes. Each of the central themes is given its swift treatment, and the whole, like a pointillist painting, becomes apparent and gains coherence when we step back and view the novel from a distance. This is a similar technique to that used by Cela in *The Hive*, although there, a slender argument and many recognizable, if not memorable, characters recurred intermittently throughout.

The style conveys an impression of choppiness through the many short sentences and the abrupt shifts of imagery. Mrs. Caldwell's speech—and this is an eminently verbal book—seems somewhat stilted and halting in Spanish. Her sentences are continually punctuated, interrupted, by terms of endearment for her son, and by qualifying, adjectival phrases. Though the chapters read smoothly enough individually, their brevity and ever-shifting focus convey a sense of impediment. Both in the sentence and in the chapter it seems as if Mrs. Caldwell's consciousness were constantly interrupting to amplify, explain, and even censor her expression.

The translation attempts to recreate the impression of choppiness and involution in Mrs. Caldwell's speech. In addition, her nationality is made evident through the choice of an English word or phrase where an American one might also fit. Anglicisms—for example, *hire-purchase plan, goods train, lift*—thus replace their American equivalents—*installment plan, freight train, elevator*. I have also been guided by the way an Englishwoman might speak about the subjects in the novel. The spelling, however, is conventionally Americanized.

At the time the translation went to press, Cela had finished revising the novel for its definitive Spanish edition, in the seventh volume of his *Obra completa*, in course of publication in Barcelona. He has kindly allowed me to incorporate certain changes and additions, among them a heretofore unpublished chapter (204) and a new prologue, which bring the translation into line with its revised version.

It is a pleasure to acknowledge the assistance of three people in the completion of this translation. My thanks go to Camilo José Cela for his great patience, and for his help in clarifying passages which my command of Spanish could not. Mrs. Amelia A. de del Río, of Barnard College, read the translation in draft and offered many useful suggestions. And my wife, Maxine, who read the novel aloud, materially aided my attempt to capture Mrs. Caldwell's psychology and tone. Obviously, the interpretation of the text and any mistakes which may exist in the translation are solely my responsibility.

J. S. BERNSTEIN

Providence, Winter of 1960—
Trumansburg, New York, Summer of 1965

Mrs. Caldwell Speaks to Her Son

BY CAMILO JOSÉ CELA

For my brother Raphael,
a student in the
School of Mining Engineers

Foreword

I met Mrs. Caldwell some time ago in Pastrana, during my trip through the Alcarria. Mrs. Caldwell was very carefully prying up the tiles in the bedroom where the Princess of Eboli died; then, one by one she wrapped them in tissue paper and put them away in the suitcase, a big-bellied valise filled with many varied and meticulously arranged things.

One day in the inn after supper, Mrs. Caldwell read me the pages she was writing in memory of her beloved son, Eliacim, who was as tender as a maidenhair-fern leaf and who died heroically in the tempestuous waters of the Aegean Sea. Essentially, the little work of Mrs. Caldwell's was entitled: "I Speak to My Dearly Beloved Son, Eliacim." She had various other titles in her notebook, but without a doubt, the most beautiful one is this one.

A month or a month and a half ago, a friend from London, the quail-castrator, Sir David Laurel Desvergers, wrote me, giving me the sad news that Mrs. Caldwell had died in the Royal Insane Asylum in that city.

With his letter, Sir David sent me a little package with Mrs. Caldwell's manuscript. "She wished," he explained, "that it be sent to you, the young vagabond with whom she became intimate to the point of weariness and almost to the point of satiety. Mrs. Caldwell always spoke of you with affection and used to explain to my wife and me that you had

5

a sweet and elusive look, very similar to that of her adored son, Eliacim Arrow Caldwell, who was as tender as a maidenhair-fern leaf, and who died heroically, as perhaps you already know, in the tempestuous waters of the Aegean Sea (Eastern Mediterranean)."

The pages that I am publishing today are those of my poor friend, Mrs. Caldwell, that wandering old lady with whom I became intimate to the point of weariness, although never to the point of satiety. May she rest in peace.

Chapter 1: I Know Very Well Why You Jump, My Little Eliacim

You came jumping along like a silly cherub, just like a cherub whose brain had been swallowed up by a moist cloud. I was already used to seeing you; your father (God rest his soul) had spent his life jumping in the most varied ways: jumping from side to side, somersaulting, doing Polish leaps, jumping like a plover in heat, and hopping endearingly. You came jumping along like a silly cherub, with incredible giant jumps.

"Let me tell you something," you said, your cheeks rosy with mirth. "Something that's enough to make you die laughing or at least rupture yourself."

But I was unmoved: "No, don't tell me anything; I have an earache."

"Your ears hurt?"

"Yes, I just told you, they hurt terribly."

Then, you shrugged your shoulders, blinked with an infinite but perhaps casual elegance, and began to whistle softly, very quietly, like a young blackbird at sunrise:

How much I want to live
Now that my ears don't hurt
And I am happy, almost completely happy!

That's what one guessed at once, as you were whistling, my faithless one, my malodorous, domestic hyena. I didn't have to be a lynx to see that.

"Can you guess what I'm going to tell you?" you asked warily.

"No."

"Well, I'm not going to tell you anything, which is worse. Not even that I don't care if your ears hurt. Time wasn't meant for feelings nor for those in pain. My ears hurt too, from time to time, and I don't tell anyone about it, unless it's you. My ears hurt me too when I have mint soup, for example, and I can't find a shoulder to cry on."

It's not fitting for civil servants, for public officials, to walk around picking their noses; it always makes them appear in a bad light. Now you're a civil servant, a public official; nevertheless, you frequently, but not too frequently, walk around picking your nose, as if you were a doctor or a Hungarian count. I shall not warn you any more. It's up to you!

All this happened one night when there was a terrible storm—do you remember? I remember very well—in the cottage at the club, when you got your position (if it hadn't been for the influence of Uncle Rosend Gerald you would never have gotten a position in your whole life, but that's another matter), and I told you that I was inviting you to spend two weeks in the mountains devoted just to relaxation and to your telling me that the pines ozonize the atmosphere, which it always pleased me so much to hear you say. Can it be possible that you don't remember?

It was when that writer, after thinking a lot about it, said, "Two huge black clouds are amusing themselves playing tennis with the lightning," and Mrs. Pyle was unfaithful to her husband, it was a funny sight to see! "The lack of air pressure," said Mr. Pyle, "is what's wrong with the mountains."

You were reading a book of verse, seated by the fire, and I

kept busy thinking of the following: "I would bestow on my little son Eliacim all the charms of Nature." (I'm sure my thought was not excessively original; and that, son, is something I would never know how to forgive you, even if I wished to, which I don't.) The upstairs world, the bedroom-limbo was much more complicated.

"Well, tell me what it is that's enough to make me die laughing, or at least to rupture myself."

You are spoiled, Eliacim, very spoiled; you've gone through life imposing your will. An employee at the club told you:

"The gentleman is wanted on the telephone."

I knew well enough that boys of your age are excessively interested in their mothers' friends. Therefore, I asked you, "Why do you drink so much, my son? If you keep up at that rate, you'll ruin your life prematurely.

Then you whistled again. Most probably, the song you were making up had lyrics more or less like these:

How I love you secretly
Oh, sweet, dearest Hortense! oh my sweetest
  Hortense Pyle!
For a kiss from your shapely mouth,
For just one kiss, even though you weren't dying
  of enthusiasm,
I would willingly turn over my whole future to you.
Tra-la-la. Tra-la-la. Tra-la-la.
Some day, can we hold hands by the light of the dim
  moon,
And whisper very short and exciting words of love in
  each other's ears,
Like tropic, for example, or lips, or golden pearl, or
  floss?

9

I think so. I am young and full of hope.
Tra-la-la. Tra-la-la. Tra-la-la.

Believe me, dear, all of this fills me with disappointment.

Chapter 2: The Music Hall

As you came in you said:

"Where is Genevieve, the Algerian mulatto? Where has that damned Genevieve hid herself? They told me that she dyed her hair gray. Do you know anything about it?"

No one answered you. The somewhat elderly woman who was with me, and who, so she said, was the wife of a cavalry colonel who had distinguished himself considerably at Dunkirk, asked me, "Do you know that handsome young man?"

Well, she didn't say handsome.

"Yes, he's my son, my only son; his name is Eliacim."

"That's funny!" she added.

Pardon me, dear, but I had to agree with everything that woman told me. I'm not going to repeat it to you because, even if it wasn't too bad, neither was it pleasant—what is usually called pleasant—for you.

Later, like a conqueror, you went off toward the bar. I thought, "Now we're sunk!" But no, fortunately, we weren't.

The cavalry colonel's wife was talkative and a little vulgar that night. She was elderly, as I've told you, but she had two enchanting green eyes, overflowing with promises that had already been fulfilled.

"My husband's name is Epiphany. Don't you think that's a

euphonious and beautiful name? My husband drinks *ojén*,* a Spanish drink which is very good for the digestion, and he's had an operation for phimosis. And yours?"

"Mine is dead. As a young man he had to be operated on for phimosis, too. When he passed away, we gave him a second-class burial, because we weren't too well-off. He, poor man, was very sorry about it. Shortly before he died, all he did was ask me, 'Don't you think we could get enough together for a first-class burial, if we borrowed some money from the man on the second floor who was always so helpful?' As you will understand, my good friend, I turned a deaf ear to all of that; you, being a married woman, will be able to understand that."

You, drinking whisky, made a rather good effect, with your new orange and blue, well-knotted tie, and those eyes that you have inherited, no doubt, from the one who was always, as your poor father used to say, so helpful, and who, had I asked him for it, surely would have put up what we needed for your poor father to have, as he deserved and as was his dying wish, a first-rate, deluxe, A-one burial.

Chapter 3: Help Me Wind Up This Skein of Cyclamen-Colored Wool

"I don't want to, I don't want to. Don't you realize whom you're asking things of, the most trifling things?"

You, son, were yellow with rage, yellow like candied yams or a brand-new wedding ring. And not because I asked

* Translator's note: *Ojén* is a Spanish brandy made of anise and sugar.

you to help me wind up that skein of cyclamen-colored wool (you had done it very willingly on other occasions), but for the seven reasons that, now that I'm no longer afraid, I will dare enumerate for you:

(Forgive me if I use Roman numerals like Müller in his *History of Greek Literature*. I know very well that it's not polite and that I should have avoided it.)

I. There's nothing doing with my friend, Rosa, in spite of her being a Majorcan; you know that as well as I do, even better than I do. Plenty of moon, plenty of hand-holding, in time plenty of 'come close to smell the flowers,' plenty of reading Samuel Taylor Coleridge's poetry. That's up to you! A mistaken strategy. If I were younger, I could even give you a demonstration. It usually works, I think, if you cover the bosom of the woman you love with daisies, her back with daisies, her thighs with daisies. Rosa! Rosa!

II. You would like to find reasons to be able to say, like your cousin Albert, "Oh, God; oh Dear God! Why do you leave me to my poor resources in such a critical moment?" But if anyone accompanied your cousin, my dear, in that difficult moment, your cousin Albert would be much less happy. He himself, on a certain occasion, confessed it with tears in his eyes: "Aunt, please, don't uncover that shoulder. . . ."

III. In spite of all your listening, it's seventy-two hours since the radio has played that song about the female gondolier with the golden curls and the profound look. It's in bad taste, but it's effective. It hurts me too, believe me.

IV. You are not certain that when I reproach you, and tell you, for example, "Why are you bent on walking zigzag so as not to step on the cracks? Don't you see that it gives rise to gossip?" I'm only thinking of your future.

V. The moon, that pale star of the night, as that funny

Minister of Transportation used to say, is not in a favorable phase.

VI. In the beer hall called "The Dragonfly of Silver Satin That Whistles, Sings, Drinks and Spreads Happiness," that Welsh village girl with the well-turned legs, who had blushing cheeks and jet-black hair, no longer serves the York ham sandwiches. Her name was . . . I don't remember her name. But I do remember that when she washed the glasses energetically, her low neckline was tight and glistening.

and VII. Your beloved sweetheart, Miss Pepper (no, I don't feel like, I don't want to call her by that ridiculous name she has), has cross-eyed feelings. When I told you this, you got mad; but now you're becoming aware of the fact that we mothers always tell the truth.

The truth is that I was not discreet in asking you to help me wind up this skein of cyclamen-colored wool that I bought, to make you a muffler to keep you from catching a cold or bronchitis now that the cold weather is coming.

Chapter 4: An Old-Time Tango

When I dance that sinister tango with you, the one that begins: "Come into my arms again, let's forget what happened," I feel like a young girl. We are nobody, my dear; nobody, absolutely nobody, darling Eliacim! With my silvered hair . . . What a horror! My bitter mouth . . . What a horror! With a dead look . . . What a horror!

Dance that tango with me, dear; press me close against you, and hum those repulsive words that give me back my youth and fill my heart with evil intentions. Obey your mother, my son, so that no one may say that you're disobedient.

Chapter 5: Tradition

You, my son, will never be entirely happy if you do not love tradition; you will only be happy for those odd moments, when, no matter how much you resist, you won't be able to help it; like a little ball which, by being stared at, takes heart and changes itself suddenly into a beetle with elytra the color of old gold.

My son, unless you love tradition, you will not see luxuriant orchids, nor, rather white lilies, growing in your heart, the lilies that make useful reputations, reputations which have their price, and make people say of those who possess them: "He's a charming boy; he's going to go places."

You, son, as long as you don't love or pretend to love tradition, will not lay the golden egg.

I'm doing my duty by warning you. Now, do what you think best.

Chapter 6: A Poker Game with No Stakes

The players were three, my son; three and you, four. The clock struck one in the morning. The bar was full of ladies and gentlemen. That American, whom some time later the police escorted to the border, began his harangue as he did every night: "Ladies and gentlemen." That sounds good, that "ladies and gentlemen." The young Duchess of Selsey was shouting that vile story about the bullfighter and the hunting dog. Admiral MacTrevose, blushing with happiness, was rubbing knees with Mrs. Stornoway, the shy redhead who gives her husband so much trouble. You, son, carried away by your poker game, were forgetting the most basic rules of celestial mechanics.

When, taking her by the wrist, you said to Mary Rose: "Pardon me, I would prefer you not to cheat," and her husband gave you that terrible punch on the mouth, I, you can believe me, was proud of you.

Chapter 7: The Bad Part Came Later

You were a tortured young man. You put on an antisocial air for people. You felt yourself to be perhaps more complex than necessary. You wrote your verses and prose without much of a knack; that's the truth. You thought, or better still, dreamed, about things with a certain pleasure, even with a certain sternness; and the very faint throbbing of a flower's petal, or the harsh sound of a butterfly of innumerable colors flying, or the look, capable of demolishing cathedrals, of a sparrow in love, or your heart, above all, your lonely heart, seemed to you like the bishops and rooks, the queen and pawns of the chess player—logical items with a purely conventional value.

The bad part came later.

Chapter 8: Cognac and Rum

In young people like you, Eliacim, there is always present, a little, the possibility of an excessive fondness for the synoptic.

I used to tell you constantly: "Always think approximately; always think in generalities; a little confusion is always convenient." But you stubbornly persisted in ignoring your elders' advice. Now, it's not so bad! you're a civil servant, a public official, and you can look out for yourself. Nevertheless, I still think you ought to modify certain of your habits. No one cuts the Christmas turkey's neck without giving him a couple of little cups of good cognac, do you understand? It's like a ceremony. The condemned prisoners also get a goblet of rum, at the proper time; it seems that it, how shall I say? cheers them up. Rum is very much a man's drink.

Chapter 9: The Dragonfly

I wish you were a dragonfly, or something as small and elegant as a dragonfly, so that I could carry you eternally near my heart.

Chapter 10: Havana Cigars

When you finished your training, even after the year of practice, when truly and with no room for any doubt you had finished your training, you took me to the park, and on a wooden bench under the old walnut tree called "The Lucky

Worm," putting on such a transcendent air that for a moment, certainly no more, I thought of a declaration of love, you said, "Are you pleased with me, mother dear?"

I was staring at some allegorical drawings that another woman and another man, some other day, had carved in the bark of the walnut tree with the point of a knife, and truthfully, I didn't know what to answer. You caught me a little unprepared.

I wanted to make amends, for I thought, "My son, who has placed all his illusions in this critical moment, deserves sweeter treatment from me, a gentler attitude." Then I said,

"Do you know which Havana cigars are the most aromatic, the most delightful, the best shaped?"

Your glance followed mine and together they settled on a heart pierced by an arrow which those lovers of a day gone by left in the bark of "The Lucky Worm," the old walnut tree, the wailing wall.

Chapter 11: Isabel

At the race track the other afternoon, you allowed yourself to be carried away by sentiment and you lost all of your money. That old Isabel deceived you with her cunning and now you have to pay the consequences. You don't learn by experience; you don't learn by experience. And it can't be because I am not, oh! constantly telling you.

That she has a graceful figure is something I already know. Also, I know that she comes from a good family, that she has good breeding, and that not long ago she had considerable success at the beaches on the Channel. It doesn't matter: I still think Isabel's being six years old is too much. And for the Two Mile, even more so.

Chapter 12: A Literary-Musical Party Including the Presence of Some Ex-Minister

It was organized with great solemnity; the truth is that you organized it with a great seriousness, very punctiliously even in the most minor details, those which frequently pass unnoticed by even the most skillful hostesses. The guests were very satisfied, the petits fours were excellent, and thank Heaven you could find some of the best Scotch whisky in time. To take any credit away from you is the furthest thing from my mind, but the truth is that everything developed very luckily.

Doing the honors, you had an unexpected easiness, a touching air, an obvious artificial grace: you seemed like an embassy secretary, a young priest, a dress designer, a perfumer, almost a *coiffeur pour dames*.

We were all enchanted to see you get up when, with a hand raised as if to say, "Here I have, dear ladies, a charming style for spring, as chic as it is simple, in which the elegance of line is not disturbed by any unnecessary element, etc.," you smiled with your most expressive and captivating smile: "Ladies and gentlemen, I am very pleased to present to you the young poet from the South, unknown to us until today, whose esthetic ideas, etc."

The young poet from the South, whose pants and jacket were a little short, whose hips were rounded and whose skin was pale, adjusted his glasses and began to recite his poetry: "I am terribly sorry to remind you, young lady, of your recurrent and unfulfilled promises of eternal love that were lost, oh! in the mist."

The corpulent ex-minister, whom everyone, to hurt his feelings, introduced by saying: "Mr. So-and-So, ex-minister of Such-and-Such," recited a hymn to the fatherland, in fourteen-syllable lines, and then gave a piano recital which was much applauded.

Since I didn't know what to do, I, son, suffered when you looked at me; I suffered horribly and inexorably.

Chapter 13: At the Pool

The obese, tremendous, monstrous women at the pool, all of them mothers, had already spent five days swimming above the drowned man. You were the one who told me about it. The water was changed every Sunday evening, and the drowned man, a boy from the provinces who lived modestly by giving voice lessons, had been there, from all the symptoms, since Monday morning. Friday afternoons, the water tastes of chlorine and has a grayish color, like dirty milk.

The obese, tremendous, monstrous women at the pool, all of them mothers, swim awkwardly, swallowing water, spitting water. In former times, how time passes! there had been abuses, many abuses; you were the one who told me. The obese, tremendous, monstrous women of the pool, all of them mothers, would stop, from time to time, and smile wondrously with an attitude whose interpretation held no doubts. You explained it to me very well, swimming around the room like a fat, charmless woman. How funny it was to see you! The management then had put some mysterious powder into the water, some powder invented by a German chemist, and when the obese, tremendous, monstrous women, all of them mothers, stopped and smiled wondrously, with an attitude that had only one interpretation, the mysterious powder went into action and a red ring formed around the women.

"It was necessary to take that heroic and shameful step," were your words, dripping with charity like a lemon.

The obese, tremendous, monstrous women of the pool, all of them mothers, spent five days swimming above the young voice teacher who had put all his hopes in conquering the city.

Well. Now, with that business of the mysterious powder, it happened that at times a woman came out of the water and went off toward the dressing rooms with her bathing suit dripping and plastered to her skin. Some got dressed and went off to take care of their homes. Others didn't. Others went in swimming again above the drowned man, over the young voice teacher who, as no one bothered to close his eyes, must certainly have looked like a young dead sea bream.

You, my son, have always seemed to me rather like a bird, a charming bird.

Chapter 14: Persistent Rain on the Panes

Rain is falling persistently on the panes, my son.

It's a bad day, and the insects, in the green, glistening meadows and the dark, green woods, are trying to find the shy hole in the rocks, the hole which overflows with clemency.

When you were about to be born, my dear, the rain wasn't falling persistently on the panes, and a radiant sun shone high in the sky while the barometer read a healthful pressure.

It was springtime, my son, and the flying insects were writing your name, with gold-colored letters, on the short, white, little clouds.

I never thought I could come to love you so much!

Chapter 14 bis: Persistent Rain on the Panes (another version)

Rain is falling persistently on the panes, Eliacim.

This is intimate and gentle weather, weather to hide ourselves inside our own hearts, within our own hearts: the hearts we could describe as burning.

I dream calmly of the idea of this weather's lasting, of its lasting and staying with us forever, just as my best and purest thoughts about you.

You, go away. I'll stay by the chimney-side, looking toward the armchair you are not to occupy. But I won't be alone, I swear to you. Your mother is not yet of an age where she has to stay alone, like a stone on the road.

. . . you, go away . . .

Chapter 15: "Criminal Court"

It was a small provincial newspaper that had funny sections, sections full of charm. I bought it every day to read your name, which was almost never in it.

The sections were called: "Ephemeris," "About Society," "Local Life," "Lives of the Saints and Religious Life," "Our City Twenty-Five Years Ago," which was the funniest section, "Around City Hall," "Hunting and Fishing," "Five Minutes of Leisure: Games and Pastimes," "Public Notices," "Poetry at Day's Dawning," which was where you sometimes came out, "Around the Kitchen," and "Criminal Court."

(People read this section on the sly as if they didn't give it too much importance.)

Chapter 16: It's Always Funny to Think about Little Children

Yes. When you were little, relatively little, and you hadn't even gotten past Archimedes' principle . . . Well, it's a rather long story. You had corkscrew curls, blond, soft and luxuriant corkscrew curls. . . . Everyone admired you, son, with your pretty, pure silk scarf, and your little brown Morocco shoes. . . .

It's a long and strange story, Eliacim darling, that I don't think ought to be told entirely.

Chapter 17: The Well-Bred Neighbor

Not you. But your cousin Richard, oh, your cousin Richard! Your cousin Richard is an idler, who does nothing but displease his mother.

Your reckless cousin Richard has a neighbor whom it would be good to stuff, when his time comes of course, so that he might join the collections in the City Museum and serve as an example for all of us. The director of the City Museum would order him to be dusted off gently and frequently, and would also have his eyes washed with egg white, those eyes that seem to ask the visitor: "Have you read the decalogue of the city-dweller?"

"City-dweller? That doesn't sound . . ."

The neighbor of your ungrateful cousin Richard has so many skills that the set of whole numbers probably wouldn't be enough to count them all. The most impressive of his abilities (well, one of the most impressive, and I'm citing it only as an example), is that trick of the surprised lift rider. Your vile cousin Richard's neighbor, when the moment is right, says with a smile on his lips, "No. The lift is weak; I'll walk up, thank you." (The only defect which might be imputed to the neighbor of that great rascal your cousin Richard is an excessive love of falsehood; the lift has tremendous power; it's one of the best and most powerful lifts that I've ever known.) The neighbor of your cousin Richard, of that scoundrel of a cousin Richard, puts the surprised lift rider into the lift, pushes the button, and runs out upstairs.

The neighbor of your cousin Richard, whom I would very gladly call a bastard if he weren't the son of a sister, always arrives in time to open the door on the third floor, on the fourth, on the fifth, and even on the sixth or seventh. He gets to the higher floors only with certain difficulty, with certain symptoms of fatigue.

He smiles, says "Oops!" and then breathes deeply.

"Do you understand, my son?" I asked you once, and I ask you again now, "Do you understand?"

Chapter 18: The Rack-Railway Train

The rack-railway train is a little train, painted white, drawn by an ancient machine named "The Spruce Forest," like the hotels for clandestine lovers, and it is driven by an old engineer dressed like an Eskimo, smoking a pipe, like a sailor.

You get into the rack-railway train with your skis on your shoulder, look for a good spot, lean out the window and say goodbye to the girls at the station who will go up later, when their boy friends come and pick them up. The rack-railway train spends all day making trips. . . .

We all spend the day somehow.

Chapter 19: Cherimoyas with Kümmel

To have cherimoyas with kümmel for desert is a mark of distinction, of great distinction. It would please me very much, my son, if any day at all in the "Apple of Discord" restaurant, so popular with the members of the Upper Chamber and their friends, you were to think, "I'm going to devote this to the memory of my dear mother," and were to ask for cherimoyas with kümmel for dessert. If you only knew how grateful I would be.

Chapter 20: Do You Want Anything from the City?

Tell me, please, whenever you go to the city. What effort is it for you? I promise to answer you always, "No, son, nothing, thank you," and even though I might need some magnesia, or darning cotton, or stamps, or new needles for the gramophone, or salt, or the latest novel by that French friend of yours who is becoming so famous, I will always tell you, always, I promise you, "No, son, etc."

Chapter 21: Flies

Perhaps someone has already studied in detail the numerous, exceedingly numerous, varieties of flies that there are. People say flies, flies, or perhaps flies, flies, flies; and with that flies, flies, or that flies, flies, flies, everything is understood.

Well, son, I think that there are at least twenty varieties of flies. I can tell you very little about this. It would be convenient for some studious entomologist to clear up these concepts for you.

Chapter 22: The Time

You, son, many years ago, cried disconsolately when, on a walk, you asked a man the time, and the man, instead of telling you "Twelve," which is the hour which children always ask, replied, "It's wah, cutie, it is almost wah."

I promised to buy you a magnificent Swiss watch where

the wah was not shown, but which would have the fi, the Indian brave, the bathing suit, the boo, the nugg, the seven and the five.

If I have never bought it for you, now you know why.

Chapter 23: Let's Get Up at Dawn to See the Sunrise, the Majestic Sunrise over the Round Old Hilltop Where the Fragrant and Timid Little Wild Flowers Grow

You told me all of this one night after dinner. I had to answer, "No, my dear, in spite of everything, no."

Chapter 24: Trout

When we used to go trout fishing in Rapid River and we spent the dead hours in silence, thinking about varied and different things, for example, how clever trout are, how ravenous, how swift, or perhaps, surely they've seen us by now, or even, it's really a beautiful day, what difference does it make if there wasn't even one trout in our creel? What a good time we had! Do you remember?

You brought a green eyeshade for the sun, and a small silver flask, with your initials, full of cognac. I used to wear a cretonne apron, one of the many different ones I have, and some dark glasses.

We used to eat underneath any little tree, and we drank

fresh water, water from a stream that sprang up at our feet, water that was perhaps too fresh, too pure. What we liked best to see, from afar, were the fat, shining bulls of Sussex, whose meat is so highly prized. Do you remember? What a good time we had!

We used to return to the city exhausted and sad, do you remember? with faint spirits and our heads under our wings.

Chapter 25: Botticellian! Botticellian!

I wish she'd die by a horrible and patient Oriental torture.

The sly one, as soon as she sees a child, even though he may really be a veritable piece of garbage, says in a loud and violent voice that pierces the eardrum, "Botticellian! Botticellian!"

She's an old teacher of whom I have very bad memories, my son; I beg you to share them with me. She doesn't smell good, but bad, and she won't admit that anyone does anything well, or properly.

If you talk about the weather, she says the weather is bad. Completely bad? Well, at least, bad for the health, or bad for farming.

If you talk about the beautiful sun shining in the sky, she says the beautiful sun shining in the sky is bad. Completely bad? Yes, without doubt; it's the kind of sun which comes before a storm. Oh! dear God, the electric sparks which kill the little shepherds of the mountain!

If you talk about Natalie, who has two deep, beautiful black eyes, she says Natalie is lewd and indecent and that you can see it in her deep, beautiful, apparently beautiful, black eyes. "Why? What has she done?" "Ah! You have to look beyond what people do or what they don't do! Why else has God given us the power of deduction?"

If you talk about the mayor, she says the mayor is a thief, potentially a thief, and that's the worst kind.

Only if she sees a child does she tremble and shout, with her raucous, shrill, barn owl's voice, "Botticellian! Botticellian!"

Now, I'm telling you that I wish her a frightful death by some slow Chinese torture.

Son, don't abandon me.

Chapter 26: A Hot-Water Bottle to Warm Your Feet

I bought it for you when you were graduated, for it didn't seem right to me for a graduate to go around with chilblains. Esperanza's boys, who were shy and had circles under their eyes, could go around with chilblains because people expected it; but you, son, not you.

You said, "The hot-water bottle is beautiful. Did it cost a lot?" At that time, prices were not so inflated, but the hot-water bottle, nevertheless, was an expensive one, a first-class hot-water bottle.

On my way home with it, I made up a poem for it. I don't remember it very well; all I know is that it began like this:

Hot-water bottle that will warm
The feet of my dear son,

Of my loved and beloved son,
Of my son who, such a short time ago! was graduated;
Will you always warm him sweetly, softly?

You already know, Eliacim, that when it's something to do with you, I get very sentimental.

Certainly there are in the world, and even in our own city, mean people who won't believe in the purity of my thoughts. Nothing matters to me; I know well enough the course I have to follow and the words I should whisper in your ear to cheer you up, when you're depressed at times.

Also, I know what kind of example is good for youth, and what kind of example is bad for youth.

Chapter 27: The Counterfeit Coin

With your counterfeit coin in your pocket, my son, you had the funny air of a counterfeiter. Counterfeiters, my son, are suspicious and sly, like scorpions or second-story maids, and at family gatherings nobody defends them, not even Uncle Albert, who, as you very well know, is a dissipated man who had a mulatto sweetheart and who still has many friends on the Continent.

When you entered the haberdasher's called "The Lancaster Shuttle" and, with your pretty counterfeit coin in your pocket, wanted to buy some garters to present to your beloved mother on her wedding anniversary, how far you were from supposing that they were going to put a hole in your counterfeit coin, piercing it on the hard counter with a wire nail!

Surely the blows must have resounded like dice in a tomb,

and you, son, always so sensitive to noise, trembled, I'm certain, like a recruit before the lace dressing gown of the colonel's wife, whose name, no doubt, is Louise.

(I ought to warn you, my son, that I imagine the lace dressing gown of the colonel's wife, née Louise MacDucaud, hanging over the back of a little armchair in the warm, half-lighted bedroom, which is deserted to the eye, but not to some one of the other senses. The colonel's wife, as you know, is young, and, so they say, somewhat temperamental. Colonel Tomlinson also is young and has a promising career; they ruin their health on the northwest Indian frontier, but they get promoted rapidly.)

Chapter 28: Letters That Come in the Post

You were glowing! How happy you became when that anonymous letter you had spent so many months waiting for came for you in the post!

Getting anonymous letters, Eliacim, was always a difficult luxury, something that not everyone can permit himself, something that is forbidden to many. Your poor father (God rest his soul) would have given anything to get an anonymous letter from time to time, and to be able to say, at the club, those things about cowardice or about the best thing being to pay no attention.

Your anonymous letter, my dear, was beautiful and exquisite. It was also threatening, gently and lightly threatening. "It's difficult," it said, "to become Colonial Secretary or president of the Board of Directors of a Bank, an oil company, or a big trust. But it's also difficult to stumble upon a naked woman eating grass in the meadow, or to live forever, or to know if a horse is a Conservative or Laborite: horses are fickle, and probably a Norman horse, fed up with sweating hours overtime on the docks, is a Laborite, and a thoroughbred, with a pedigree in Gotha's *Almanach*, who won the Derby twice, is a Conservative."

Getting anonymous letters, son, is as difficult, or almost as difficult, as becoming Colonial Secretary or president of the Board of Directors of a Bank, an oil company, or a big trust. Nevertheless, it is easier than finding a naked woman eating grass in a meadow or than living forever, or at least for more than five hundred years.

Chapter 29: Soup

"Should one have soup?" Or "Should one not have soup?"

On the first assumption, "What sort of soup should one have? Should one have creamed Argenteuil, creamed Longchamps? Should one have Colbert consommé, Mille Fanti consommé? Should one have oxtail soup?"

Oh, my son, how ignorant men are when it comes to soup! I would like to see many a great man (men who've passed into history in standard-sized type), thinking about this thing which, poor me! I wish to explain so clearly to you.

I have a great deal of affection for your memory, don't I? But in spite of everything, I cannot tell you anything useful about soup.

Chapter 30: Thoughts on the Tunnel

When the train goes into the tunnel, my son, like an arm that enters the sleeve of a dress coat, all the travelers try to adopt nonchalant postures, like the dead, postures that say, "Don't think that tunnels frighten me, no; tunnels leave me cold, as if nothing were happening."

The smokers slowly bring their cigarettes to their mouths so that we all may see that the little light is not shaking, that the little light has a Spartan steadiness; and the nonsmokers who before, in the trains of old, had a special compartment completely full of hoarseness, try to clear their throats with indifference as if to say, "But sir, please, is it possible that you can think the darkness terrifies us?"

(Only the girls of marriageable age who are scatterbrains and have a shiver up their spines go into the tunnel with a hopeful and shamefaced blush, and come out of the tunnel pale and filled with a feigned despair, as if they were trying to pretend to be girls who were just embraced for the first time.)

It's very curious, my dear, very curious and instructive, to observe how, when the train enters the tunnel, all the passengers adopt well-studied postures like the dead.

Chapter 31: Black Silk Lingerie

I remember well, Eliacim, my darling, my little wild rosebud, my delicious, tart, country strawberry, my son, that when I used to get dressed and undressed before your graduation photograph, in which you were already a man, you always looked displeased at seeing my black silk lingerie against my white skin.

(Since you died so young, son, you could have permitted yourself a certain lack of respect which I never would have thrown back in your face.)

I swear to you, my dear, that I could never think that all that had any malice in it at all. I swear, likewise, that I am lying. Just one hint from you would have been enough for me to discard my black silk lingerie forever, which would have been exchanged item by item for silk lingerie of pastel shades adorned with a simple little bit of white lace.

Would that please you more? How foolish I've been!

I respect all points of view, son, absolutely all. Experience tells me that you men, on certain questions, have your own private and different points of view.

Chapter 32: Your Personal Papers

When my fate decreed, love, that your body should disappear in the delicate weeping of the sea, I went through your personal papers with my heart in my mouth. What terrible times!

I have been, son, the sole cause of your shyness. You very much loved all that I taught you to love, and the idea of continuing to love frightened you. I could have suspected that.

You, son, now it's time to tell you this, became shy in adolescence when your voice changed. (Please, I beg of you, don't insist about the causes of your shyness with that now useless cruelty.) How sad, my son! Make a real effort not to blame me.

Some other time (but I can't guarantee it) I'll continue with your personal papers; I can't do it now.

Chapter 33: Is Work a Sin?

It's a thought that has always worried me, son, because I've always been afraid of falling into heresy.

I think that the love of work, my son, not work, is a grave sin, and I tried to bring you up according to this idea.

Man was not created to work, but to be idle and not eat of the forbidden tree. Only when he sinned and was expelled from Paradise, he found that he had to earn his living with the sweat of his brow.

Let's not love Jehovah's curses. Let's not fall into blasphemy.

Chapter 34: The Money Instinct

The money instinct, my son, the instinct which lifts the people, is hard to come by.

No one studies to be a millionaire, Eliacim, just as no one studies to be a poet; one studies to become an economist, or a professor of rhetoric, but that way one dies poor and uninspired.

The poet pulls blushing clouds out of everything he touches; the millionaire converts stones into gold nuggets.

It's useless to plan to become a millionaire or a poet. And vocation isn't enough. Intelligence isn't required. Industry is a wild virtue, like a bird without eyes. But one does need the instinct, the difficult instincts of poetry and money.

The love instinct, dear, is of another order. Neither you nor I had it, or else we had it so well hidden that it wasn't of any use to us.

Chapter 35: The Roulette Wheel at That Seaside Resort That Resembled Paul Valéry's "Graveyard by the Sea"

You said, "Double on fifteen," in a low voice, and in a loud, almost stentorian voice, "Zeno, Zeno the cruel, Zeno of Elea!"

That exquisite Scandinavian, Ilsa Sündersen, hardly took her eyes off you; her husband kept reproaching her, and then as if to make it up to you, she played the same number as you.

That seaside resort, I don't know why, had a vague but obvious resemblance to the "Graveyard by the Sea" of Paul Valéry.

Chapter 36: Veronal

It was always the elegant thing to do, my son, to commit suicide with Veronal. It's a suicide for people, for example, who have loved a lot, for people who've never lacked anything, absolutely anything.

Their souls progressively take on an opalescence and an uncertain air, and their bodies languish, little by little, with an elegant sadness, with a studied and pleasing abandon.

Veronal, my son, ought to be taken with champagne, and at night, like resignation.

Women, after taking their Veronal, can allow themselves to be loved by a passionate and respectful lover, by a slow and obliging lover; that is proper. What is not proper, my dear, is the writing of farewell notes.

Chapter 37: Down

It is something which perhaps it will be found that Walt Whitman praised, when the revision of all his manuscripts is completed. The edition of Pelligrini and Cudahy, of New York, is good, no doubt; but in it, my son, the verses in which W. Wh. surely sang the praises of down are missing.

2.

Or perhaps W. Wh. didn't sing of down at all: of that emotion we get from big, old pillows, from infinite numbers of downy legs, from anonymous fuzzes whose stories still have not been told. God only knows!

Chapter 38: A Trip about the Bed

Do you remember, my son, how entertaining and touching the trip about the bed was?

That nightgown that I won in the Spencers' raffle, that dull-orange nightgown that you liked so much despite its being, no doubt, a little in bad taste, a little bit in the Dutch taste—I only put it on on very special days, on your poor father's (God rest his soul) anniversaries, or on those other days when we decided to have a go at that silly game of chance of the trips about the bed.

You, who were still not educated enough so as to be able to understand things without having to explain them completely, used to get as red as a beet and tried to hide your emotion.

Chapter 39: Summer

Summer is the season of people who are dying, the season in which the dying clamber aboard the train of death which goes by, rhythmically whistling old tunes of yesteryear.

In the summer, children feel like accursed birds, and married women come up with some beauties in the ancient art of behaving well in their husbands' absences, each one in her own particular way. .

One cannot believe that summer could be that time of wonderful weather of which some poets of scant inspiration sing.

Faith, my son, is to believe what one has not seen. You have already seen the summer, but I don't know if you've seen it as it is, the way I assure you it is.

You ought to believe that in this, as in everything, I am telling you the truth and nothing but the truth.

Chapter 40: The Sea, A Sea, That Sea

The sea is a word that makes me nauseated; it's something I can't talk about calmly. The sea is a beautiful and intolerable young girl who's had life too easy.

A sea, any sea at all, even though it be a specific, definite sea, is never anything. A sea, a love, a donkey, a velvety flower, a child lost in a big city, an employee mercilessly persecuted by his boss, a bullet that goes flying across a battle sky. All this is very vague, very imprecise. Perhaps what happens is that everything needs a name.

Ah, but the things with concrete names also have their drawbacks! That prophetic love that was called Pyramid;

that sinister and disagreeable donkey that turned his head when he heard the name Catullus pronounced; that flower christened Strange Hope; that child who was lost because no one said to him: Give me your hand, Richard Henriques; that employee who at home was called Hateful, and in the office, Pity; or that impudent bullet, Daisy, which eagerly sought out the pancreas of the battalion's tenderest recruit. The name of the Aegean Sea (Eastern Mediterranean) is a name I don't want to pronounce. Or, at least, a name I want to pronounce as little as possible, like a distressing obligation from which I constantly wish to flee.

Chapter 41: The Dead, and Other Equally Vain Thoughts

The dead are wont to assume surprising positions, my son. Probably, if they could see themselves, they would be the first ones to be surprised. Possibly a long and detailed study of the postures that people adopt in death would be interesting. Their posture could be classified into three groups, and beside each one of the groups would stand a tender, domestic animal, frozen stiff; a hen, a barnyard rabbit, a duck, a small, soft and grunting suckling pig. If people were more cultured than they are, dear Eliacim, it would be known already, at this late date, which posture would be the preferred one for each person when his moment arrived. Your poor father (God rest his soul) preferred, my dear, the charitable posture of a cat that has just given birth. It was funny to see him. Some friends had to help me stretch him out in order to put him in the coffin.

Various vain thoughts can find lodging in one at the end of the day; one has only to pay a certain amount of attention. A locket with a golden curl, a child who's not yet been beaten, another child, wise in the ways of the golden oriole's flight. A multitude, a multitude of them!

Chapter 42: Lord Macaulay

I always loved you very much, my dearest; I always esteemed you with my most egoistical and sincere affection; for me, you have always been something like the goal of all my aspirations. But I would have preferred to see you calm and circumspect like Lord Macaulay, elegant, conservative, and an expert in English history.

Perhaps it's my fault, and nobody else's, that you haven't been a Lord Macaulay. Your father had very little part in you—he made a very minor contribution; only we mothers have children, and shelter you, always with our own thoughts, wrapped up in a whole cloud of violent and fertile loves that cannot be confessed. The father, your father, my dear, was never more than a decorative element, the excuse for our being able to love, in the son, all his virtues: those which have form and those which don't; those which have a name and those which don't; those which serve for something, and those which, strange as it may seem, also serve for something.

Lord Macaulay, my son, would have played a great role as your mother. As your father, he wouldn't have done any more than fulfill his obligation. But time, Eliacim, is something I have not yet discovered a way to fight against.

Chapter 43: Monarchies

It's amusing to think about monarchies. One can throw oneself down on a sofa and begin to think, like an Indian priest: I am beginning to lose my toes, I no longer feel my toes; my foot has fallen off up to the ankle, my leg ends at the ankle; my calf dissolves like sugar, how well-off we are without calves! my thighs are disappearing just like a ship sailing away on the sea, it's comfortable to feel oneself without thighs; the monarchy shades off like a subtle little cloud, resting in a strange limbo without a compass and without a watch.

Let us defend our own monarchy for it is the last stronghold of our heart. The heart is not in the breast, but rather fixed in the most recondite and veiled part of our monarchies.

Let us not stubbornly defend the obdurate, the hardhearted king. A monarchy is something which is not inherent in the person of the king. But a monarchy no doubt needs a king; a king that can make our insatiable heart pulse toward a certain objective.

Chapter 44: Italy, France, Spain, Our Old England

In Italy, mothers love their sons always feeling a little like very beautiful and violent Beatrices.

Maternal love in sweet and concrete France is usually an instructive spectacle filled with remote reservations. Madame Bovary was an immaculate mother.

In far-off Spain, mothers bite their sons on the neck, drawing blood, to demonstrate their tenacious, unchanging love; so Mr. Borrows who went around vast Castille, selling Bibles, so he tells us, according to what Mrs. Perkins says, that witty woman who killed her husband by giving him an irrigation of nitric acid diluted with water.

In our old England, mothers have no definite and foreseen way of loving their sons. In this, as in many other things, there exists a great freedom.

Chapter 45: I Love the Spanish Deck

I love the Spanish deck, the deck of the clubs, cups, spades, and golds. It's more moving and also more poetic to play cards with the Spanish deck.

Any one of the cards from the Spanish deck is an inexhaustible hatchery of suggestions, all of them cordial, caressing and friendly. With the Spanish deck, the deepest veins of the nape of the neck perspire with a delightful and exceedingly fine perspiration, a perspiration that only the elite are usually aware of.

You never felt any great attraction for the Spanish deck, and I, no matter how much I urged you to love it, never got more than evasiveness and effrontery. Truly you have been a boy of very slight precocity in your glandular development.

Chapter 46: Urban Planning

People go around these days exceedingly occupied with what they call, a little mysteriously, urban planning.

In some countries, my son, Urbana is a woman's name. Women who are called Urbana are not usually beautiful, but on the other hand, they do have charitable sentiments, kind reactions, lasting affections, and principles of great strength.

This business of urban planning doesn't make much sense. The planners could make an unequivocal gesture of sensibility by killing their leisure time becoming adept in the useful skills of Isaac Walton, the perfect fisherman. Perhaps that way the streets and squares of the city would come to be designed with a greater sincerity. Everything is possible.

Chapter 47: The Hourglass

It was entertaining to watch time pass through the little neck of the hourglass.

When I write these lines in your memory, Eliacim, it is Monday. The hourglass doesn't keep the days of the week—it's a very small hourglass; but I know that it's Monday, I'm certain that it's Monday, and no one could get it out of my head that right now, it is precisely Monday.

At times I feel myself dying, on Mondays especially, invaded by a vague and exceedingly strong desire to live three or four days in advance, Thursday or Friday for example. Then I tell myself: today, no doubt, is already Thursday. Although I want to live till Thursday and I'm almost certain I will achieve this, I imagine that it's Monday; but this fantasy of mine is only an error. Then I look at the calendar and the newspaper's dateline, and I see that the calendar and the newspaper's dateline suffer from the same mistake, the same hallucination as I do. Then I go out into the street and ask some good-looking woman: "Would you be so kind, madam, as to inform me of what day of the week today is?" The woman replies: "With pleasure; today, my friend, is Monday, Monday all day; tomorrow will be Tuesday; day after, Wednesday; the next day, Thursday, and so on in order."

The common belief that all Mondays are Monday is very widespread. It would be much more beautiful if part of mankind argued strongly that some Mondays are Thursdays.

Perhaps if the U.N. ordered public hourglasses to be built, ones capable of keeping the days of the week, and the months of the year, this could be achieved.

As long as an heroic and almost revolutionary step is not taken, I'll go on bound to the rack of being unable to decide for myself in which day of the week I'm living, and in which day of the week I want to live.

This, my son, is not free will.

Chapter 48: Solitude

For some time now, my dear, I've thought that the strictest solitude could reflect your shadow on things. But it wasn't true. Your shadow, at times, appeared, yes, but in a blurred fashion, dulled of all charm.

I can get to seize you, your memory, better, son, among men, animals and things, among minerals, mountain birds and the plants in the garden. Perhaps this doesn't seem bad to you. I swear to you that I do all of this only to be able to feel you closer to me, more on top of me.

Solitude, my dearest, is not a good wood for passing my fingertips over the imprint of your name, Eliacim.

Chapter 49: Winters in the Greenhouse

Can you imagine, dear Eliacim, the pleasant, the boring winters of the tulip bulbs in the lukewarm and moist greenhouse, in the luxuriant greenhouse.

Sometimes I think, my son, that I would like to change into a little fistful of greenhouse dung, or into that endearing spider with long and hairy legs, that hangs improbably from his web which shines impudently at the sun.

At other times, on the other hand, I am tempted to destroy the greenhouse, destroy it wildly, in order to rejoice among its ruins, in order to stroll barefoot over its broken glass, its broken bricks, over the miraculous and whole tulip bulbs.

Chapter 50: That Bald Skull We Carry Within Although We May Try Not to Remember It

I was always brought up with the idea that skulls are dry like the holm oaks on the mountain which the lightning kills.

And my presumption was punished by God's condemning

me to keep you in mind, my dear, with your skull turned into a nuptial chamber for the jellyfish.

But this idea doesn't console me either, Eliacim; you have a mother who is very little resigned to things.

Chapter 51: I Would Like to Compose a Poem

I would like to compose a poem in your honor, a poem in which the most beautiful and meaningful words would fit: child, gray, despair, cautious flight, legs, sacrifice, feeling, caramel, the nearby horizon, goodbye.

If I had any talent, Eliacim, I would compose a poem in your memory, a poem in which the most beautiful and meaningful words would fit: adolescent, gray, unpardonable, impudent flight, thighs, agony, love, dry fruit, horizon in the hand, goodbye forever.

Chapter 52: The Skin, That Seismograph

When the human race manages not to feel too vile, it will use the skin, that great invention, for a seismograph.

For my part, my son, I can tell you that I feel very happy when a shiver runs up my spine, or when the light hair on my arms stands on end, or when I notice a chill and somewhat rough skin brushing across my temples.

Then I understand that a tiny, blind fish comes out of your eyes.

Chapter 53: Without a Mask, without a Glove, without a Shirt

Thus, Eliacim, the most honorable heroes, those who, like you, preferred to give to the ocean fish what we earthly mothers didn't know how to keep for ourselves.

Oh! if I were a bristly and violent fish of the deep, or a very fine grain of sand from the bottom, or salt!

Without a mask, without a glove, without a mask, one can also die, Eliacim, without pain or glory. And dragging along even the sins that were not committed, the oldest and sweetest sins, those sins which would have been able to transform us into sounding boards, who knows if not into a caressing little music box.

Chapter 54: The Little Country Flowers

I would like to have begun, when I was still young, and if not beautiful at least in bloom, back around the time when you came along, without any surprise, into the world, a well-ordered collection of little country flowers.

Exquisitely dried and pinned down, each one on its sheet of deckle-edged paper, the collection of my little country flowers could now fill a whole cabinet, a miraculous cabinet.

I, now that I am so alone, would pass my time away with my collection, like a gravedigger, imagining violent and abortive championships of floral love, which is, perhaps, the cruelest and most condemned of all loves.

With my cabinet inhabited by evil thoughts, my son, the world wouldn't be painted so white a color as it is for me today. And you, perhaps, would peek out from behind the daisy, or from underneath the virtuous furze.

If I had a complete collection of little country flowers, Eliacim, I would travel to the sea which cradles you, to drop it, suddenly, into the waves.

But I didn't remember in time.

Chapter 55: The Devil's Presence

When I was a little girl, the devil appeared to me almost every night. The devil, in order to appear to me, adopted the most various forms. Sometimes he pretended to be a tiny cinnamon-colored dog which smelled of jasmine; other times, a minute black spider, the flavor of mint; other times, a light trembling on the wall that shone like a firefly; other times, like your grandfather, Eliacim, who had a corpulent presence but a high-pitched voice.

My father, my dear, had always been very unfortunate, because, although he was very happy, he couldn't believe it. When he came to give me his blessing at night, and a kiss on my forehead, he smelled intensely of sulphur.

I, at that time, my son, was so ingenuous, that I imagined myself the daughter of the devil. When I thought about it, with my eyes tightly shut, I felt a little hot flush running across my breast like a centipede gone mad.

Later, things changed a lot.

Chapter 56: On Foot? On Horseback? By Bicycle? By Stagecoach? By Car? On Board a Luxurious Transatlantic Steamer? On the Train? By Plane?

To search for you, Eliacim, to be able to go to jail for you, I would not waste my time deciding.

When one loves with the firm disillusionment with which I love you, my darling, one doesn't waste time or energy; that's reserved for lovers whose clock still rings the hours of illusion.

To look for you, Eliacim, to give rise to gossip on your account, I would not give away to anyone even one minute, that minute which afterward no one could return to me.

I don't know how you must see things. What I can assure you of is that, in my position, you wouldn't see things in a very different light than I do.

Chapter 57: Slang

If I knew how to speak slang well, no one would be able to hear one single word from me except in slang.

If I could debase my tongue, I would never again move it for virtue's sake.

Slang, my son, is a little bit like that black-sheep relative whom all envy and all pretend to despise.

I would have wanted for you, Eliacim, a life of slang.

(Don't pay much attention to me either; perhaps it's just something that we mothers, whose sons died gloriously in the fulfillment of their duty, say.)

Chapter 58: Sailing

If you and I lived in the days of sailing ships, oh! if you and I lived!

In the sailing days, the sea resembled a bedroom in which—what a shame to have been born too late!—you and I would have met!

It might have been that upon seeing each other, we would not have known what to say to each other. For these moments of indecision, the gods created the sense of smell, which is somewhat like the radar of the soul.

In the sailing days, Eliacim, the sea pretended to be a forest of amorous trails, a jungle which had lost its virginity for love.

Today, no longer.

Chapter 59: Notions of Architecture

The counterpoint arch, dear Eliacim, is an easy arch to recognize, but it is not simplicity which I, at least at this moment, want for you.

With certain notions of architecture, my son, a man like you is capable of showing himself to be irresistible with women of the most various ages, even with the old ones like me.

The horseshoe arch, dear Eliacim, is an elegant and dangerous arch. But it isn't elegance, although it is danger, that I want for you, at least when I imagine you as I would have liked to have you.

With certain notions of architecture, my son, a man like you drowns in the weeping of the women he destroyed

49

forever, of the women who couldn't look him in the eye. Not anything else, absolutely: such was its power.

The ogive arch, dear Eliacim, is a handy and genteel arch. But among many other things, it's not charity or gentility that I would have needed from you.

With certain notions of architecture, my son, a man like you lives with his soul nourished by love.

The truth is that you, Eliacim, never had any elementary notions about architecture. You, Eliacim, were rather a deserter.

Chapter 60: Animals Set Free

Can you imagine, my son, the animals of the mountain set free, the destructive pests, and the meek and sentimental little beasts, wolf and marten, buck and chamois, viper and linnet?

Can you imagine, my son, the healthful gabble on the mountain, with all its animals set free, with all their hearts beating without restraint?

At the bottom of the sea, my dear, the fish enjoy an even greater liberty, a more silent, more intimate freedom, a freedom more of their own.

I wish I was a dirty octopus of the deep, my darling, so I could embrace you, so I could say into your ear: now you will no longer be able to escape. Even though I know very well that you were not to hear, that you always played deaf to the words of your mother, Eliacim.

And also I would like, what vain pretension! to be a siren on the cliff, my son, to be able to recite Homer to you or, at least, to please you a little.

Chapter 60 bis: Animals Set Free (another version)

If you were an animal set free, Eliacim, a weasel, a mole, a cricket, a vulture, I would pursue you mercilessly; I would pursue you with dogs, with traps, with poison, with the most accurate death-dealing weapons. Everything, Eliacim, before permitting you to escape again, like a shameful sea gull, over the paths which the sea washes away, mercilessly, every morning.

But you, my son, are not an animal set free. I beg your pardon for not having known how to make of you a free animal, a sparrow, a fleet stag, a hare.

Chapter 61: The Collapse of the Mark in the Other War

In Switzerland, in the Scandinavian countries, in Spain, and also in many other places, there was a multitude of people who were ruined by the collapse of the mark in the other war. That seemed like the end of the world.

The thought that bank notes can give such frights fascinates me; the frights that I had in my life were of a very different order.

And I'm still waiting, Eliacim, for the last one.

Chapter 62: The Small Polished Pebbles
That the Water Carries Along

In the mountain streams, Eliacim, the water runs along carrying polished and well-washed little pebbles, white, black, blue, red, it depends.

The insects that fly over the waters, the transparent dragonfly, the orthodox butterfly, or those that rock themselves in the rushes on the shore, the maternal spider, the monstrous and fierce praying mantis, look, with wonderment, at the polished little colored pebbles that live in the river bed, and in their unknown language call them by names which in ours mean diamond, jet, sapphire, ruby.

The little polished pebbles that the water carries along, Eliacim, are the image of fiction, the shining shadow of fiction. I told you this one day, with no success, thinking a little bit that knowing it would enable you to take the proper precautions.

But you disobeyed me.

Chapter 63: The Sundial

The sundial has living hours, hours of the working day, and dead hours, hours of vacation and idleness.

The sundial serves to mark the hours with fidelity, without allowing itself any compromise.

The sundial doesn't run fast or slow, and it outlives the man who built it, and all of his kin.

The sundial knows no sickness or death. Sickness for the

sundial is not damage: it's an earthquake. Its death, Eliacim, would be the death of the sun.

The sundial always offers excessive security.

Chapter 64: Business

From their young childhood, my son, some men can catch the delicate and persistent smell of business. It's an ability like any other of the precocious abilities.

The young businessman, when in his heart the bush which bears the fruit that is bought and sold first begins to flower, discerns remote, difficult and complex signs that lead him, like a sleepwalker or like an initiate, to the most elastic and variable goals, those which are rarely achieved.

In the family, when a businessman is born, the ceilings are painted green, so that the whole city may know of the event, and an extra-large ration is given to the carrier pigeons which, tired of coming and going, took refuge like ghosts in the belfry.

In our house, my dear, the ceilings were never painted green. Your poor father (God rest his soul) had very ordinary and commonplace ideas about the color of the rooms. And that's the way things went with us.

Chapter 65: Events

There are very important people, Eliacim, people whose importance is real and not pretended and tolerated, who are excessively fond of events, accidents, derailments, rapes and murders.

I can understand, my dear, how this can be. Events are like the filling that cures the cavities that burrow into the simple souls of the taxpayers. Without events, my son, without their beneficent presence, thousands and thousands of men would feel themselves perishing daily, lulled by a soft and quotidian conjugal neighing, by a soft and quotidian filial neighing.

You, son, who in your day were also an event, although certainly nothing more than a collective event, can put down on the credit side of your ledger many, a great many throbs of satisfaction.

There are people of undoubted importance, Eliacim, well-known and respected people who occupy, more or less rightly, executive positions and positions of responsibility, who are excessively fond of events, poisonings, shipwrecks, spectacular holdups, the delicate and almost chemical business of espionage.

Chapter 66: Shipwrights

The shipwrights sing, while they're working, the beautiful sea songs that please the summer visitors so much, songs of monotonous rhythm, an almost briny rhythm.

The shipwrights, Eliacim dear, resemble industrious and happy coffinmakers, disciplined and jubilant artificers of solid boxes for the dead.

When I see them working eagerly, my son, although with rather a relaxed eagerness, such vain and childish thoughts occur to me that I almost do not dare tell them to you for fear that you will scold me.

But on the arm of a shipwright, Eliacim, your mother, right now, would feel very happy walking along the seashore and seeing how the sea gulls take off with a fish with shining scales in their red beaks, toward the black rocks, the green, cold rocks of the coast, the wet rocks that throw atrocious shadows on the ash-colored clouds.

It's possible that there is some tune entitled "The Caulker's Sweetheart." I don't know it, but everything is possible.

Chapter 67: Cacti

The cactus flowers did not get wet in the waters of the Great Flood. In other words: the cactus flowers retain, with the same devotion as that with which they might preserve a relic, the thick dust of the Old Testament.

I am awed by the idea that God may punish me for my various sins, transforming me into a fleshy bristly cactus leaf, into a perennial and lonely cactus leaf.

If such were the case, my darling, I would give all the little I have and am so that a cataclysm such as had never been remembered would carry me, even if in pieces, to the bottom of the sea.

If not, not. The evil we know is better, the evil which comes to be familiar to us.

The flowers of the cactus, Eliacim, live submerged in a limbo which knows no weeping.

Chapter 68: Fine Glass Beads

I have one dress embroidered with blue beads and another with green beads. According to the thoughts I get out of bed with, that's how I choose my dress. My system works all right.

You, Eliacim, one could notice at once, harbored in your heart a great fondness for fine glass beads, a great fondness in embryo, a great fondness that never took root, perhaps because of a lack of time.

I believe that the ancients, the truly wise of ancient times, also felt attracted by fine glass beads, by the little beads of pleasant colors with which I adorn my dresses, those dresses that I select, each morning, according to the thoughts with which I get up.

When I get up thinking of you, Eliacim, I put on the dress embroidered with blue beads. And when I get up thinking of you, my dear, I put on the dress embroidered with green beads.

Chapter 69: Eldest Sons

Your poor father (God rest his soul), Eliacim, had been the eldest son in his family: it was something one noticed in him at once, something that he couldn't have hidden even if he had tried.

Eldest sons, Eliacim, at times even in spite of themselves, usually carry a dark spot painted on their foreheads, which darkens their spirit and will: to be an eldest son is one of the most dangerous tasks that can fall to a man.

In some countries, Eliacim, in some with ancient cultures, the eldest sons in each family gather on the mountain at dawn, summoned by the hunting horn which the devil sounds, and they masturbate painfully until they feel themselves at death's door; there are documents which prove this conclusively.

The old men of the outskirts of the city, on the day the Spring is born, go to the mountain with their eyes blindfolded, and choose by lot any eldest son, an eldest son who is thrown from the highest rock, amid the guffaws of his companions and the distant tears of the young girls who pray for his soul while the bells toll for the dead.

The customs that are still extant in some countries with ancient cultures are, Eliacim, very curious.

Chapter 70: Summer in the City

Summer, my son, is the season of the city, the triumph of the city. I would have liked to summer with you in a city that wasn't ours, in a hotel in which there were almost no rooms left, in a hotel full of shy, withdrawn pairs of newlyweds. Now I see very clearly that so much happiness would be too much to ask, but what do you want? Neither do I see why I must renounce everything.

Summer, contrary to what people think, is the time of the city, the occasion that the city awaits—with what a bitter resignation, sometimes—to strip itself bare and show its charms and scars.

Do you remember, Eliacim, what a good time we had that summer when we didn't leave the city, at Mr. Mennant's bachelor supper, that funny man from Singapore? Do you remember the bullfighting lessons that M. Jacques Tourneville, from Carcassonne, gave us? Do you also remember how poorly that soprano, Fiorella dei Campi, that plump lady who emptied a bottle of seltzer on Sir Edward Harriman, held her gin?

Yes, my son, summer is the mirror of the city, the city's wet nurse, the apotheosis of the city. Since people aren't brave enough to know it, they flee the city in summer.

Chapter 71: The Mine

The miner, Eliacim, keeps his thoughts in the deep well from which he comes up daily, to weep out his disgust over the afternoon's light. You disappeared too young, Eliacim, to realize perfectly the most elementary things, those things that have their key in maturity.

If some time, a woman in her prime were to ask me, just for example, Is your son Eliacim interested in the mining question, I would reply, looking her in the face defiantly: I don't know; my son and I, madam, do not usually talk of such topics, believe me.

The air in the mine, Eliacim, tastes like an ancient drugstore or like an herb garden, and also like a hand that has been kept for many years in a chest. You disappeared so young, Eliacim, that you didn't come to master the little science of tastes, that little science whose emblem is disillusion.

Ah! But if some time a swallow should ask me, let's say, "Is your son, Eliacim, interested in the mining question?" I would reply, looking him gratefully in the face: "Yes, without doubt; my son, Eliacim, confessed it to me one day when he held me by the hand more than half an hour, in a little neighborhood cafe."

Minerals in the mine, Eliacim, can be of three classes: diamond, gold, and coal. It's not certain that there are tin mines.

Chapter 72: Water in the Fountain

You came in with a very firm step, Eliacim, and said: "With the water in the fountain you can do real miracles." "Oh yes?" replied that somewhat consumptive girl with whom you were flirting (I'm referring to Miss Stadford, the sister of Captain Stadford). "Yes, real and unexpected miracles." "Which ones?" "I'll tell you: ablutions and gargles." "Ah, I thought you were referring, Eliacim, to the playing of the water in the fountain." "Yes, that too, I meant to refer to the playing of the water in the fountain too; what happened is that you didn't give me time." "Pardon me." "You are forgiven." "May I ask you something, Eliacim?" You, my son, smiled with a great sweetness to say no.

(It would be embarrassing to go on in such detail with the utterly commonplace story of your flirtation.)

Chapter 73: Cattle in the Barn

The cattle in the barn is lined up like the children in school or the troops in the barracks. The cows, to the cowboy, are all the same: like the children for the teacher, and the soldiers for the captain. But this is a lie, my dear, a great lie, an abject and cruel lie. What difference does it make!

The cattle in the barn exhibits such a tranquility that visitors of average intelligence shiver with fear at seeing it. The same thing happens with the children in school, and with the soldiers in the barracks. The meek, son, the resigned, the silent, keep in their hearts the intact little bags of hatred, the stored reserves of the hatred with which they dream of blinding us one day.

The cattle in the barn, Eliacim, is lined up like men waiting for the firing squad.

Chapter 74: The Ancestral Customs of Tibet

You were reading, with great care, my dear son, a book on the ancestral customs of Tibet, a copiously illustrated book. I like to remember you absorbed in attentively contemplating the walls of Lhasa.

Young people like you, my son, are losing their affection for instructive travel books, the diaries of explorers, and prefer to repeat the foolishness of poets. Poets don't collect in their poetry, Eliacim, the ancestral customs of Tibet.

I can assure you, my son, that love in its most various manifestations also figures among the ancestral customs of Tibet. I was never in Tibet, Eliacim, not even anywhere near it, but you can be sure of what I am telling you: a Spaniard named Sebastian Rico, who was somewhat related to the Dalai Lama, told it to me. Sebastian Rico had beautiful black eyes, eyes incapable of lying. I, my son, was in love with him for some time, although the truth is that my love was never returned, at least not returned entirely.

Chapter 75: Vegetarian Cuisine

Vegetarian cuisine has great partisans in vast sectors of public opinion. I, especially, think vegetarian cuisine is good for entrees, although not for anything after the entree. We would need five stomachs, Eliacim: a rumen, a reticulum, an omasum, an abomasum and a fifth stomach with no name, to be able to say that vegetarian cuisine is completely good, good for the palate, for the nerves, for the muscles and good for the soul.

Vegetarian cuisine, my son, breaks down at the start: man needs to poison himself, Eliacim, in order to know he's a man. Man is a poisoned animal, perhaps the only poisoned animal.

Vegetarian cuisine, son, is an abdication, it is taking away from life the fear of all vengeances, that moving heart beat, that isochronous beat.

In broad sectors of public opinion, vegetarian cuisine has many partisans. But it doesn't matter.

Chapter 76: A River Collection

Your Uncle Albert had a great collection of rivers. He devoted Sunday mornings to his magnificent river collection and spent the time talking on the telephone and trading the rivers he had doubles of. The Nile, Danube, Amazon, Volga, Mississippi, were the most common rivers, the rivers that the beginner, the young collector, found first. On the other hand, the Escalda, Saar, Po, Tordera, Zambezi, were difficult rivers, rivers that were found in the collections of your Uncle Albert, President Roosevelt, King Farouk and very few others.

Your Uncle Albert died without seeing his life's dream come true, the International Federation of Fluvioteques (I.F.F.), with headquarters in London. Your Uncle Albert had always been a dreamer.

Almost all the river collectors the world over sent representatives to his funeral; the eternal dissenters—there are always some—did not. The moment of closing the coffin was one of great emotion—all the rivers of the world wept.

(Our family, my son, is decimated by fatality. Your Uncle Albert left his river collection to me in his will. I don't know what to do with it and I wish I could consult you. Perhaps the wisest thing would be to set each river free, I don't know. The rivers of the world would run in their beds shouting: Mrs. Caldwell is our Abraham Lincoln, Mrs. Caldwell is our Abraham Lincoln!)

Chapter 77: I Hate with All My Heart

There are so many things that I detest with all my heart, my dear son, so many things that I abhor with all my heart, that it would be very difficult for me to be able to enumerate them for you. It is a real blessing to feel alive and in good health so as to be able to devote a few hours a day to detesting something with all one's heart. The only thing I regret is that you cannot accompany me.

Detesting with all one's heart, Eliacim, detesting deeply, attentively, carefully, without a chance for distraction or boredom, is something which is not granted to everyone, something which requires a patient and even sacrificial training.

Your mother, my dearest, detests with all her heart everything that surrounds her: the air that she breathes, the maid who washes the dishes, the cat that allows itself to be petted, the water that she drinks, the bread she eats, the comfortable teapot, the radio programs, the cigarette that burns without reproach, the coming and going of travel, the familiar furniture.

It would be more comfortable for both of us, Eliacim, if I enumerated for you the things I hate but not with all my heart. We would finish sooner and I would have more time to continue hating with all my heart.

The only thing that saddens me, I've already told you this before, is that you cannot accompany me. But there are things we can't do anything about.

Chapter 78: The Legacy of Our Elders

That which is called the legacy of our elders, my son, that which people call the legacy of our elders, Eliacim, is usually an entelechy without too much meaning. What keeps on happening is that no one wants to say so, something I can understand, although not excuse, because it's more comfortable to continue the way we're going.

The legacy of our elders, my son, is a phrase to be said with a cold mouth and with a hand resting on one's breast. Phrases that compromise little—religion, family, or the legacy of our elders, or the unity of Europe—ought always to be said with a cold mouth and with a hand on one's diaphragm. It's not worth while to wear yourself out.

When I was a little girl, Eliacim, and grandpapa, little grandpapa, said "the legacy of our elders," it always upset my digestion. Some days, when he repeated it two or three times, it was even necessary to call the doctor. The doctor, this is the truth, didn't pay much attention to me: he preferred to talk to grandpapa about the legacy of our elders.

One of the first times I deceived your poor father (God rest his soul), I felt a great and hard-to-explain remorse of conscience, because my lover, an elegant Calabrian horseman whose name was Carlo Dominici, spoke to me, with what inconsiderateness, Good Lord! about the legacy of our elders, of the imperishable bequest of our elders.

Now that I'm old, or almost old, Eliacim, it occurs to me at times, to think, although fortunately not more than briefly, about the legacy of our elders. I am comforted, nevertheless, by the idea, although it doesn't compensate me in any way, that I have not given anyone or anything, absolutely to no one nor to anything, the opportunity to say, as if nothing had happened, that stuff about the legacy of our elders, which one must intone with a distracted air, cold-bloodedly and with a hand in a noble attitude.

Chapter 79: Rooming Houses

Noisy, frozen, damned, humble, fragrant rooming houses are like the little wrinkled white flag of someone who surrenders unconditionally, of one who surrenders suspecting that magnanimity which does not exist.

In rooming houses, my dear, the strongest and most lasting alliances are established between the most apparently disparate stomachs: it's the old law fulfilling itself, inexorably, for the enjoyment of the lodgers, the faithful spectators of misery.

If I had the nerve, Eliacim, I would rule with an iron hand a rooming house full of pale people, undernourished, dying guests whom I would try to treat badly. But I haven't the nerve—I'm no longer at all young—now I can aspire to few things.

Chapter 80: Benjamin Disraeli

How far-off now, Eliacim, are the times of Benjamin Disraeli, and his beautiful dress coats.

When I go out into the street and come across sailors in uniform, men who wear your own shroud, I feel as if I'm living by some rare and undeserved miracle.

When Benjamin Disraeli was an adolescent and neither you nor I had been born, the world was no more unhappy than it is today. I would have liked to have the strength of a Benjamin Disraeli to have gotten from the Crown an entire series of not-at-all concrete prohibitions which perhaps would have helped to make me happier without you.

Surely the maxims of Benjamin Disraeli have been published in a beautiful volume.

Chapter 81: The Accordionist

I knew a leprous accordionist who carried the worms of his sores in a box made of rock crystal. He dressed in green and red and wore earrings of gold that ended in a bell. He had been born in the hottest of the Portuguese colonies, and according to what people said, he was the son of the only case within memory of the old sin of bestiality having been fertile. (It seems that his mother, who was the daughter of a trafficker in opium and precious stones, was possessed by a shark that had all the sailors that crossed that distant sea terrorized.)

When I recall the leprous accordionist, Eliacim, I see him always with your own face, with your own smile painted on his purple lips. It's an idea that attacks me when the days dawn too brightly and the city seems unknown, just as if it had been rejuvenated suddenly, by all the young men who traded it for the bottle-green depths.

Chapter 82: Miriam, the Lyrist

Playing the lyre, Eliacim, is a task for delicate spirits; it would have pleased me very much, had it been possible for you, if you had married Miriam, the lyrist.

I know she is rather repulsive, that she has a glass eye, although one of very good quality; I know she's in poor health, and that she's around sixty, but, what does it matter to you, if you're dead?

Playing the lyre, Eliacim, is for exquisite souls, beings who live with a colored butterfly tattooed on their brow; I would never have been displeased at having a daughter-in-law who would spend the long winter nights playing the lyre, seated on some carmine, velvet cushions.

Humanity is losing its fondness for the noble pastime of lyre playing and this thought produces in me a deep sorrow.

Isn't it true, Eliacim, that if it were possible for you, you would oblige your mother and have many children with Miriam, the lyrist?

I am going to tell her that.

Chapter 83: Institutions That Regulate the Relations between Man and Woman

In spite of what I've told you in the preceding chapter, Eliacim, marriage, in itself, is not good. The case of your marriage with Miriam, the lyrist, is somewhat different.

Marriage is dirty and impure; the perfect state of man and woman is being engaged. Marriage kills love, or at least, wounds it gravely.

The blame is the legislators', as it usually happens, who permit natural fecundation.

Chapter 84: Tropical Fruits

My son, I am going to give you, what a thrill! a pair of pajamas embroidered all over with tropical fruits, with bananas, cherimoyas, kakis.

With your pajamas of tropical fruits, Eliacim, you can be something rather similar to a bird of Paradise.

I can't manage to explain how those mothers who have the good fortune which, you understand, I'm lacking, do not dress their sons, so that they may sleep happily, in tropical fruits, in exceedingly sweet, cloying tropical fruits.

You, Eliacim, in my position, wouldn't you do the same?

Chapter 85: The Supercompass

What great stupidity! The day will come, Eliacim, when man will invent the supercompass, a hysterical little needle that will point off many more norths than necessary. It all ends up being, my son, a problem of not knowing how to orient ourselves with the norths, scarce or abundant, that we have at our disposal.

In the midst of everything, it's a stroke of luck for me to know that you will never go into a precision instrument shop to buy a supercompass with your savings.

It will be my small vengeance against the despondent mothers, who, in their blindness, feel happy at being able to be grandmothers.

The supercompass, Eliacim dear, will come to be a grave sin of which we shall never know how to repent.

And if not, time will tell. You'll see.

Chapter 86: Goods Trains

Tired, almost human, snorting, the goods trains with their oxen for the slaughterhouse, their briquettes, their agricultural machinery, their refrigerated cars full of fish, go through the country and over the bridges sowing the hearts of children with the tiny sparks of hope.

Chapter 87: Clouds

If I saw you appear among the clouds, Eliacim, with some wings well sewed to your back, like an angel, and even with a magic wand in your hand, like a fairy, I should probably go mad from sadness.

The clouds, my son, with their soft mounds, and their movable bases, hold indecipherable theorems whose discussion is not healthy for men. Do you recall that tower-climber, who one hazy day, climbed, one by one, all the clouds in the sky and disappeared forever? According to the shepherds in the mountains who saw him, he had an empty head and in his skull were hatching the tiny little eggs of storms, the tiny little eggs which, when they break open, astonish the world.

Clouds, Eliacim, are formed by the souls of those who die on the gallows and also by the souls of little children who sin before their time. Thus, in sunny countries, sometimes inexplicable things, mysterious and very painful, inexplicable things happen.

If I saw you appear among the clouds, Eliacim, I am sure that I should go mad from sadness. It is not as an angel that I want you, my dear. Nor as an inhabitant of the white cloud, the gray cloud, the black cloud.

It is in a much simpler and more impossible way.

Chapter 88: Colored Pencils

All the colored pencils in the world, my son, were lighting up with all the colors of the rainbow, and still there were colors left over.

With the easiest colors to invent, Eliacim, pure and identifiable colors, the pencils which were to be used by the littlest children were lighting up, the almost edible pencils which manage to change, by dint of passing over and back across the paper, into the wings of a duck and into the wounding eyes of a stag.

In the depths of the sky, Eliacim, where all things are

rather a vague, faded blue tone, one can still see the ruins of the first colored-pencil factory that ever was, a small factory where some old bearded men, dressed like the German artisans of the Middle Ages, still work among the stones which have fallen to the ground.

(The box of colored pencils that I gave you on your birthday, Eliacim, since it was a box of colored pencils that was never to be used, had, instead of colored pencils, mother-of-pearl, marine shells, a stuffed hummingbird, and two or three bouquets of violets. I cried a great deal when I put the box of colored pencils on your pillow, Eliacim, dear.)

Chapter 89: Chrysanthemums

The chrysanthemum's flowers are not odious, but neither are they likable. Chrysanthemum flowers, Eliacim, enclose within their petals the most indestructible and permanent atoms of the hearts of the samurais.

Mothers who take flowers to the graves of their dead sons, Eliacim, always pick chrysanthemums, because they are the flower of company, the stinking flower that can harmonize with grief like a worm.

In the gardens where chrysanthemums are born, to be beheaded at the right time, my son, the little snail in which grief takes refuge also resides, the little empty crock in which grief hangs its "To Let" sign.

If you could only see, Eliacim, how difficult it is to come to understand the sharp chant of the chrysanthemum, above all when it's in heat! Thick volumes have been written on the topic, but none of them arrives at even fairly approximate conclusions.

Chapter 90: An Ordinary Excursion

1.

When you went on an excursion, my son, any excursion at all, and you felt like an explorer in the Himalayas, or like a staunch supporter of the most neglected science, I, Eliacim, began to tremble simply thinking of your return, which was usually a real catastrophe.

You returned from your excursions, my son, even though the excursion was just any old excursion and hadn't the slightest importance, worn out, in a bad mood, and with your features distorted, your hair and pulse out of order, your eyes shining with fever, and with your clothing torn.

But I never said anything to you, Eliacim; I was always very respectful toward defeat.

2.

Or rather. When your ears became more transparent than ever, my son, and around your head appeared the halo which preceded the excursions, Eliacim, I smiled inwardly, with a smile which I never wanted to take for a sincere one, because I knew how much excursions meant to youth.

But I was silent, I was always silent, come what might. Some of us mothers have the ability to put on the most abject ignorance concerning the results of excursions.

Chapter 91: Premarital Education

Premarital education, Eliacim, is still not sufficiently on the rise. And premarital education, my dear, especially the premarital education of the woman, even touching on pornography, is of an importance not even suspected by our rulers.

With feminine premarital education, my dear, brides would distinguish the shapes of the clouds, would know the rare laws of the prices of securities, they would be capable of doing the most common somersaults, they would predict the weather with no greater error than farmers, and they would be, in everything, the complement of that unfortunate friend, always so devoid of accomplishments, that all husbands have.

The premarital education of the woman, Eliacim, has still not reached its culmination. But we should think that this gap will be filled some day, perhaps not too far off.

When this occurs, my son, married couples will burn with delight, like haystacks, with exceedingly high flames, giving off thousands and thousands of sparks of seven-colored fire. It will be a very great and very happy day for mankind, Eliacim.

Chapter 92: Sunglasses

With your sunglasses, Eliacim, with those glasses in which you were as funny as a Frenchman, I had a great disappointment the day I lost them on the bus.

I, Eliacim, always carried your sunglasses with me to caress them, and pass them carefully over my cheeks, and over my eyelids, when no one was watching; and one day, the other day, I lost them in an inexplicable way, in a way which filled me with grief and depression.

(This is understandable, Eliacim, easily understandable since everything is straining and fighting to separate us, to cut the weak ties, which could still unite us. I wish I had the aplomb, which no one had in our home, my son, so as to feel stronger in the battle.)

With your sunglasses, Eliacim, you were not beautiful, but you were symptomatic.

I suffered great annoyance the day that I lost them on the bus, a great disappointment for which I could blame many people, although I don't.

Chapter 93: Swimming Class

Even had I had, from the time I was a girl, a daily swimming class, my son, I don't think that by now, I would know how to swim. Perhaps this ignorance of mine, this nonability, is better nevertheless, since with a little effort, it could take me much more rapidly to the place where you are waiting for me.

Some of what worries me most, Eliacim, is remembering your good swimming style, your speed, your endurance. A swimmer in the middle of the sea, my son, a real swimmer, with a special tragic effort, could play the difficult part of Tantalus to perfection.

On a map, Eliacim, the Aegean Sea is full of burning nails, full of planks run aground.

Excuse me if I go on to something else.

Chapter 94: Riding Class

Would you like to be, Eliacim, a daring and jovial seahorse jockey, to run, with the wind at your back, in the Sea-horse Derby? Oh, if I were only a mermaid, a sea breeze,

73

sea sand, a drop of sea water, a female octopus, or a female dolphin, so as to be able to buy all the sea horses on sale and make them run, with you and your companions on their backs, so that you would always win, Eliacim!

This idea fascinates me so, dear, that from tomorrow on I am going to apply myself to the riding class which up till now I've taken without any enthusiasm, like an old ring which one tolerates. And if I get to deserve my riding master's praise, Eliacim, I promise you I shall do the unspeakable thing so that the Admiralty will offer a cup which I shall win every year, come what may, in order to give it you full of little white and golden flowers.

Yes, Eliacim, it is good training, and healthy, the riding class I take each morning so as to feel a bit like an enchanted princess.

Chapter 95: Fencing Class

My left breast hurts, my dear, from my knowing that it is marked so with chalk. My fencing master, Eliacim, with his foil in his hand, is a veritable automatic machine when it comes to marking the left breasts of his female pupils, regardless of our ages.

Ever since in charity orphanages, Eliacim, they have been training poor children in the handling of gentlemen's weapons, the world has been much more confused and upset, much more careless and haphazard: even though, without looking into it more closely, it might appear to the contrary.

The fencing classes that I take, my son, bring a great disorientation to my spirit. At times, I think that I have my head in my left breast, and I suddenly stop thinking. These are very happy moments, but they don't last long. At other times, on the other hand, I think that I have my left breast in my head, and that my fencing master is going to put out my eyes.

Chapter 96: Convertible Furniture

You know very well, Eliacim, that convertible furniture, the furniture which does as well for one person as for another, is more practical than elegant, more useful than showy, or graceful, or solid. The same thing happens with convertible animals, chickens, sheep dogs, and with convertible people too: the Germans, the Americans.

You, my son, who had been brought up in relative comfort, were an avowed enemy of convertible furniture, of sofa-beds, of step-stools, of folding-chair-tables, etc., and you would not admit that many people, haunted by the pale specter that lives in empty pockets, commissioned their cabinetmakers to make a washstand-wailing-wall, or a dresser-chimney-of-hope, for example.

I know now that your position was the one that corresponded to the dictates of good taste, but, what would it have cost you to have been somewhat more charitable?

Convertible furniture, my son, like convertible animals and people, like convertible minerals and vegetables, like convertible climates and landscapes, like convertible lovers and allegiances, are the gold nuggets which can still be gotten with great effort, from the worn-out gold mine, which, in better times, made happy the men who did not need to convert themselves into convertible men.

But today, things have changed a lot, Eliacim.

Chapter 97: Captive Balloons

If you asked me, Eliacim, I would be capable of clambering up the guiderope, up to the highest of the captive balloons, up to that balloon which seemed no more than a little pencil dot between two clouds, in the very middle of the sky.

I would put on men's trousers so I could manage more freely, and I would wear a wide-brimmed hat, so the wind would be able to push me upward.

It should be pleasing, my son, to see the world from a captive balloon, to see it so far away that it might even seem like another captive balloon, bigger yes, but perhaps, even more captive. Who knows!

If you asked it of me, son, I would be capable of ruining my hands, as I say, so that you could make me out to be higher and clumsier than the highest and clumsiest birds.

Chapter 98: The Maternal Instinct

The maternal instinct, my dearest, is something much less abstruse than people think, something much easier, perhaps, to guess than to understand. The maternal instinct, Eliacim, often disguises itself with gilt powder, or with smoke, so as not to have to show its face shamelessly. The maternal instinct, my son, is something which it seems suitable to hide, something which should be watched with modesty.

The spider, my dear, which is, among all animals, the one who most acutely displays the maternal instinct, frequently disguises herself as a prairie flower or as a forest deer so as not to be obliged to have to explain her strange customs at every step.

Among women, Eliacim, and your mother has been one for some years now, the maternal instinct keeps hiding beneath the opaque varnish of good breeding. This is probably bad, but that's the way it is.

I noticed, don't tell anyone, that I couldn't escape from the maternal instinct, the very day you wore long trousers for the first time, a gray Prince of Wales trouser in which you were resplendent.

Up till then, I had always thought that the maternal instinct was a topic for the use of lower-middle-class married women.

Chapter 99: Deluxe Dogs

I would like to be a deluxe dog, Eliacim, a dreamy poodle, a daring fox terrier, a sentimental basset, a withdrawn Scottish terrier, an adventurous pointer, a snappish Pekinese, an indolent Russian greyhound, so as not to have to stand the idea of having to get dressed up in order to receive the condolences of my best and oldest friends for your desertion.

Deluxe dogs, my son, are very much removed from all social conveniences; they live very much on the borderline of all these ties which bind the mothers of heroes.

And if I were a deluxe dog, Eliacim, a capricious lap dog, I would be able to give myself shamelessly to poisonous drugs, to the most maddening elixirs, without fearing gossip, which is the thing which restrains me now. We'll soon see for how much longer.

Chapter 100: Sport

Sport strengthens the muscles, tones the soul, blunts the intelligence. Or rather: sport ruins physiology, softens the spirit, sharpens judgment.

As you may understand, Eliacim, I'm not going to waste my time, time which, on the other hand, I have too much of and don't know what to do with, in clarifying what I think may go on being confused for all eternity.

If you had been a sportsman, my son, a real champion in the sport which you might have preferred to choose, surely without my daring to influence you in favor of this or that one, perhaps I would not think as I now do. But the possibility did not arise, Eliacim, as you know.

Chapter 101: Cooked Crayfish

Stony, vermillion, inscrutable, the cooked crayfish, Eliacim, sleep the dawns of their eternal sleep in the leafy fountain of the restaurant's window. There are days when I wake up with a craving, who knows if an unhealthy one, to breakfast on all the cooked crayfish I might find in the city. I go into the street, in very high spirits at first; then, deflating little by little, I always end up taking a cup of warm tea. Why is this?

The first hours of the morning, Eliacim, are good for lonely men and women, the men and women who, as the day grows and rises, feel growing and arising in ourselves that cavern with jagged edges through which happiness escaped from us: that feeling which sleeps, sunken in some spot.

There are days, nevertheless, in which we lonely men and

women dream of revolt and we want to breakfast on cooked crayfish. What happens is, that, later, we cannot get down more than a cup of warm tea.

Chapter 102: Wine and Beer

I will never drink wine or beer, you used to tell me, I will never waste my money in working my own ruin. Later, pretending not to know the most intimate whisper of wine, my dear, although I know very well that, fortunately, your vain words did not correspond to the truth, you disappeared from my side, leaving to me, at the very edges of the place you occupied in our house, the almost invisible shadow of the hours which I should have devoted to drunkenness. I don't want to make converts.

On the other hand, Eliacim, you loved almost indecently the pleasures which ought to have been most hidden to a young man of your principles, to a young naval officer. I still don't want to make converts.

I don't think it's a sign of superiority to deprecate women systematically, or at least, out of vanity. And to pretend to, Eliacim, even less. Think that on occasions—few occasions it is true—the woman who feels herself deprecated may be the one who permits you to deprecate her. Or to love her, who knows!

You were not on the right road there, my son, although I could quote by heart half a dozen names that would make you tremble. And you shielded yourself with your vain speeches about wine and beer, with the ingenuous theories that no one even halfway grown up could listen to without smiling.

But I don't want to blame you, Eliacim; I make myself responsible for all your points of view, including the most inconsistent. To know how to be a good loser is the fate of some women who are already old. Oh, what a shame!

Chapter 103: The Amusing Young Ladies of Down, the Fresh Young Ladies of Antrim, the Merry Young Ladies of Londonderry, the Coquettish Young Ladies of Tyrone, Always So Amiable, the Smiling Young Ladies of Armagh, the Jolly Young Ladies of Fermanagh, Who Keep Those Very Beloved English Traditions, Come What May, in Ulster

To you, daughters, goes all my affection. If Eliacim were alive, I would introduce you to him so that he might take you out dancing.

Chapter 104: Mrs. Sherwood's Three Daughters

Eliacim, do you remember, Mrs. Sherwood's three daughters, so skinny, so talkative, so inclined to fall in love, got the measles: Mary at thirty, Elizabeth at thirty-two, and Kate at thirty-four. How funny it was to see Mrs. Sherwood putting little red shades on the light bulbs in the girls' room! Do you remember?

Your uncle Albert, you can't remember this, wanted to have married you to one of Mrs. Sherwood's daughters, any one of whom was ten years older than you. With which, Albert? With any one, what difference does it make to you? All three are industrious, all three are chaste, all three are well bred. Yes, I told him, those three are old enough to be spinsters, those three are nothing but skin and bones, all three are ugly and sickly. Fine, so what? Your uncle Albert, Eliacim, worrying about his rivers, was a man who didn't listen to reason, a man who lived on the moon.

Mrs. Sherwood's three daughters, Eliacim, went out walking, Saturday afternoons, ahead of their mother. Mr. Sherwood had been living for many years in the Transvaal. Mining business? some women used to ask Mrs. Sherwood. For Heaven's sake, no! Mrs. Sherwood replied, Miss Dolores Fragoso, a very beautiful Portuguese; do you want to see her picture? Then Mrs. Sherwood opened her pocketbook and showed a photo of Dolores Fragoso, autographed. Miss Dolores Fragoso was the opposite of any of Mrs. Sherwood's daughters.

Mary, Elizabeth, and Kate Sherwood were proud that their father had important mining business in the Transvaal.

Chapter 105: Top Hats

It's a real shame women can't wear top hats, like lords. If some woman would break the ice, Eliacim, I would quickly follow her; the top hat is a mark of great elegance, of great elegance which is becoming lost.

Your poor father (God rest his soul) had two top hats, my son, even if he hardly ever wore them. A man's wardrobe is not complete if it's lacking a top hat, even though the man might later die of old age without having had the opportunity of wearing it except very rarely.

The top hat, Eliacim, enhances the figure of a man, gives him elegance, endows him with nattiness, lends him majesty. If all men went about in top hats, Eliacim, there would be no wars, and you could be by my side, listening to the advice which I beg you, at least, to consider.

Chapter 106: Pleasant Phrases

I would like to have a wide repertory of pleasant phrases, my son, so as to learn them by heart well, and to be able to say them to you, one by one, until you were exhausted with hearing pleasant phrases, fed up with hearing pleasant phrases.

There are people, Eliacim, who are characterized by their pleasant phrases. On occasion, these pleasant phrases are fitting, and on occasion, these pleasant phrases come out spontaneously and out of place. But it doesn't matter, they say them as if fulfilling a difficult duty, and they smile afterward, with a sparkle of immense peace shining in their eyes.

If I knew three or four pleasant phrases, and could get to speak them with naturalness, Eliacim, rest assured that I would say them to you each morning. For one slight smile of yours, Eliacim dear, what wouldn't I be capable of doing?

Chapter 107: Seal Hunters

With their turned-down hats, their rain wear, their rude pipes, the seal hunters, Eliacim, take their own pictures on the icebergs, with a gesture of infinite cruelty, their lances in their hands and their feet on the dead seal.

To me, Eliacim, seal hunters are not in the least nice, those hard men who furiously pursue those very tender animals.

Among all hunters, Eliacim, the seal hunter is the most cunning and horrid, the one with the most hardened feelings. I think, my son, that seal hunting is a grave sin, a sin which stains the breast with an oily and sticky soot.

Because the seals, son, allow themselves to be killed like the early Christians, without one bad gesture, without even one rebellious movement.

(Perhaps this is not as I tell it to you, Eliacim; but realize that a mother ought never excuse seal hunters.)

Chapter 108: Inexplicable Fears

The worst fears, my son, are inexplicable fears, the fears without rhyme or reason, the fears without a beginning or an end, the fears which come from within, which are born in the blood and not in the air: fear of darkness, fear of loneliness, fear of time, the fears which can't be avoided because their substance is our own and most intimate substance.

I, my son, always felt a fondness for the children who die of fear, for the children who dream horrible and confused nightmares, for the children who are terrorized by the idea of being transformed into a statue of salt, by the idea of turning into a forgotten and hard and solitary vein of mountain quartz.

And if I had a lot of money, Eliacim, if I had thousands and thousands of pounds, I would spend all or almost all of it commissioning demons and death masks to terrify the children of the city, the children who see fear dyed and polished to a familiar shade.

You, my son, when you were a little child, lived in constant fear, your eyes inhabited by atrocious and permanent inexplicable fears.

Chapter 109: That Charity Raffle in Which Hope Always Flourishes

It might happen that you won a prize, Eliacim, a cake of soap, an electric sewing machine, perhaps; but most often, as usually happens, you didn't win anything; raffles exist so that hope may flourish, but not so that it may bear fruit.

When I pass that charity raffle in which hope always flourishes, my son, I usually leave some coins in the box. In exchange, they give me some tiny papers all folded up, some papers folded with great care, where it might say: you have won an electric sewing machine, but where it usually says: with your donation you are helping hope to flourish in poor homes.

In the city, Eliacim, a great love of playing, as if offhandedly, the charity raffle, in which hope always flourishes, has awakened. Our neighbors approach the raffle reservedly, they buy their little papers, and adopt a conventional and smiling air in order to lose. At times, the players forget, for a few moments, their conventional air, and wrinkle their brows slightly or permit their hands to tremble.

People, Eliacim, play the raffle, that charity raffle in which hope always flourishes, with a blind faith in their luck, with an unlimited confidence that the electric sewing machine, for example, is to be precisely for them. I always had a lot of luck, you usually hear, I have always been a darling of fortune. In this way, my son, the asthmatics, the deformed, the cripples, the ulcerous, the dwarfs, tend to express themselves. But later, when they hurriedly unfold the little paper which, often, is usually stuck together too well, they smile nervously, because on the paper, instead of saying: you have won an electric sewing machine, it says, almost lovingly: with your donation you are helping hope to flourish in poor homes.

As for me, Eliacim, it doesn't seem a bad thing for hope to flourish in poor homes. Neither does it seem like a good thing. In any case, for hope to flourish, etc., is a subversion of values.

In spite of everything, I usually leave some coins in the raffle box; also, it might happen that the electric sewing machine was meant for me.

Chapter 110: Family Life

For me, Eliacim, the business of family life is over. For you also. You can see that we weren't destined by Providence to have a family life, to stop after dinner talking and talking about the oil problem, or playing forfeits, or drinking a little glass of liqueur, or writing to a distant and circumspect aunt who is going to have a birthday and takes it very poorly if one doesn't write her a few lines of congratulations.

Believe me, my son, when I tell you that I don't at all miss family life. It is possible that one is not well-off alone; but neither is one, living in a family. Family life, Eliacim, dissolves families, it is the drug that makes families stupid.

If I were afraid to demoralize you, my dear, I wouldn't speak with you of the touchy subject of family life.

Chapter 111: Bronze Paperweights

Depicting mythological, literary, or historical characters, Eliacim, bronze paperweights enter some homes from which they never leave. It would be interesting if some thinker were to speak to us about the era of the bronze paperweights, that silent time, solemn and stiff, my dear, in which domestic, and even official, pride, depended on, and still continues to depend on, the size, the sheen, and the weight of the bronze paperweight.

In our house, Eliacim, ever since your absence, my son, everything, even the most superfluous thing, such as a bronze paperweight, is missing. Our house, Eliacim, in its present situation, is a little like the modest budget of that young poet who went through life with holes in his shoes because he only earned enough for his vices.

When I have, how seldom! some spark of optimism, some rapture of hope, which usually lasts less than the death of the drowned, Eliacim, I think that sometime the black thunderheads on the horizon may tear apart to allow, like a luminous apparition, a very comforting bronze paperweight, depicting Ganymede or the erotic and so restful rape of Europa, to come through.

But when I return, with my ears downcast, to the sad and everyday reality, Eliacim, I realize that I have been born at the wrong time, and that I was born too late for the era of the bronze paperweights which depicted mythological, literary, or historical characters.

Chapter 112: The Clock Which Runs the City

The clock which runs the city, my son, has stopped, perhaps of old age, but the city has continued running with an imperceptible and perhaps healthful disorder.

The clock which runs the city from its high tower, my son, refused to go beyond seven thirty, the hour which lovers await to cover their faces with a disguise and lift a cold waxen hand to their hearts.

The clock which runs the city from the high tower which overlooks the rooftops, Eliacim, has died, as the birds, sailboats, clandestine sweethearts, lone wolves, the hermits of Onan, the glass in mirrors, die, with infinite discretion.

(Over the embalmed cadaver of our clock, Eliacim, of the clock which no longer runs the city, the dauntless sparrows, the daring witches of the city, refuse to fly. Perhaps it is a sad omen, my son, an omen even sadder than reality, the silent death of our clock.)

Chapter 113: The Pigeons

White, ash color, coffee color, the pigeons, Eliacim, fly about over our heads, living in their world of cruel air currents, their limbo of dense and leaden clouds, their paradise of blue-green mountains with harshly drawn peaks.

The pigeons, my dear, the odious pigeons, the egoistical and ancient pigeons, beat the air with no consideration, with a contemptuous confidence, as if the air were theirs, and they go flying off, in groups of five or six, over the roofs of the houses, the roofs of the hospitals, the metallic roofs of the fruit and vegetable markets, the meat markets, the fish markets.

The pigeons, Eliacim, also fly over the fountains, over the rivers, over the lakes, over the ocean, poisoning the waters and nailing the children who were looking at themselves, absorbed, in the water, to the ground with long invisible pins.

In a better world, Eliacim, in a more just and reasonable world, the pigeons would live on deserted and distant islands, on islands which it would be very difficult to reach and impossible to return from, on islands which would resemble immense wings, cut off and white, without a tree or one single animal.

But if that happy world came about, Eliacim, if that world were to displace ours, as sad as it is, the garrets of the world would overflow with splinters, and with the ruinous dust of aborted plans, of intentions which could live only in our atmosphere.

Which would be no solution either, my son.

Chapter 114: China and Crystal

You entered the china and glassware shop with a firm step, with such a firm step that the shelves where the china and glassware objects awaited their fate shook, and you said, with a certain authoritative gesture: "Deliver to my house a set of fine crystal for twelve, and a decorated china platter big enough to hold a roast lamb of approximately ten or twelve pounds with some room to spare."

The china, Eliacim, and glassware with which you filled the house each time you brought guests home, which happened, around that time, with a certain frequency, were lined up, when things returned to normal, in the pantry, and they made a relatively dazzling effect.

Our maid at that time, Eliacim, that young widow who eloped, in the end, with an Italian miner, told me one day:

"Madam, my sweetheart told me to ask Madam's permission to sing a few tarantellas in the pantry. I allowed myself to tell him, Madam, about the beautiful appearance the pantry presented with the china and crystal objects which, lately, Madam's son had acquired, and my sweetheart said, 'Oh, Lucia' (my sweetheart, Madam, always calls me Lucia, Lucia Gigli, and sometimes also Lucia Cechi), 'I would be very happy if your mistress would allow me to sing some tarantellas in her pantry, accompanying myself on the lute, or at least, on the bandore. Will you please tell her that?' I am doing my duty, letting you know, Madam, and begging you to accede to his request."

I told her yes, my son, but the Italian miner, when the appointed day arrived, couldn't come. Our maid at that time,

Eliacim, told me that he had been attacked by a very bother-some case of scabies.

And our china and glassware, your china and glassware, Eliacim, grew old in silence.

Chapter 115: The Lawyer without Cases

I took my case to him, Eliacim, to that lawyer without cases, because I thought he would have more free time. The lawyer without cases received me very nicely, my son, and he told me straight off: "I, Madam, am a lawyer without cases; who could have recommended to you that I take on your case?" "No one," I replied; "it was a decision I made by myself; I have no one to counsel me or give me legal advice." "Are you that much alone?" "Well, yes, very much alone; the truth is that I couldn't be more alone than I am." "With those eyes?" "Enough!"

Don't think me bristly, Eliacim; you know that I'm not; but understand that I had not gone to see the lawyer without cases so that he could make love to me.

"Madam," continued the lawyer without cases, "I beg your pardon; there has been a misunderstanding, I didn't want to annoy you, I would never have dared. Let's see, what is your trouble?" Eliacim, there was a moment in which I felt a great remorse of conscience. No, for goodness' sake, who's talking about that now? "If you could see how alone I am!" The lawyer without cases got up and said: "Ah, I see!" Then he came toward me, took me in his arms, and gave me a prolonged and knowing kiss on the mouth. I thought, Eliacim, I would faint. With my eyes closed, Elia-cim, I dedicated a silent and most affectionate prayer to you.

The lawyer without cases, my dear, had a fine grayish moustache, and two eyes the color of disillusion which he half closed unpleasantly. He also had a pair of pearl gray spats and a tie of discreet and nicely matching colors.

The lawyer without cases, my dearest, according to what he told me, had been very unfortunate with women. That gave me a laughing fit, Eliacim, but I tried to hide it so as not to throw everything away. "But, how is it possible?" I asked him. "I don't know, Madam," he replied, looking into my eyes; "I have never been able to figure it out; but it's certainly true that I've never tried. Women, with exceptions, among whom I wish to include you" (he kissed me again, although with less passion), "are usually excessively logical in their reactions. Realize, Madam, that it is neither easy, nor pleasant, to be lucky with ordinary women." "Really!" I answered. The lawyer without cases, and I, my son, laughed a lot and embraced. Then, he uncorked a bottle of champagne and put a rhythmical waltz on the phonograph, a rhythmical waltz that we danced with our faces very close together. I never saw him again, Eliacim, but I swear to you that the lawyer without cases was an enchanting man, a true and complete gentleman.

Chapter 116: Courtesy

Ever since men became courteous, my son, and I'm making this small observation at a time when men are beginning not to be, things began to go much worse, all over the world. It's even a shame that this is so; but that is a question that doesn't concern us, Eliacim; let's not deceive ourselves.

Courtesy is a costly vice, my son, which, nonetheless, men don't want to renounce. The ages of courtesy, Eliacim, are usually precursors of ages of hunger, of times in which nettles and brambles are born in the frozen armpits of men.

When you began to have the use of reason, Eliacim, and even before, I tried to make you see and respect the most elemental laws of courtesy, those which adorn youth with their useless brilliancy. You, my son, were always docile; that's the truth, and my labor was not painful for me, although, at times, I carried it out without a great deal of faith.

Courtesy, Eliacim, is like the hydrangea, or like the taste of the most jaunty colored fish, those which resemble birds that have escaped from a Japanese etching, a most beautiful fraud which shines as sterilely as the starry skies.

I would not wish, not even for a moment, my son, that you throw to the winds the rules of courtesy, the usages of courtesy. Nor is this, surely, something I'm begging of you on my knees or which I would make you swear to.

Chapter 117: Pamela Caldwell

Your cousin, Pamela Caldwell, Eliacim, has married, against everybody's wishes, Mr. John S. Peace, the center forward of Fulham. Her husband, a little before the wedding, days before the wedding, met me in the street and said to me, while he offered to accompany me shopping:

"Mrs. Caldwell, I know more than well enough that I am not well thought of by your family. But my love for Pamela, ma'am, is very great and no one will be able to oppose it. Furthermore, Pamela is a girl of uncommendable habits; a girl whom it would not be too easy for her parents to marry off; you understand me now."

I preferred not to understand him, Eliacim, and I let him continue:

"Nor am I unaware, ma'am, that a soccer player, just that, no more, is very little to aspire to Pamela's hand, but I can assure you, ma'am, and I am not saying it for you to repeat, that I am something more, or at least, I aspire to something more than a soccer player, just that and no more. I have published poetry, ma'am, and I have, among my papers, a letter from Mr. T. S. Eliot, which I will show you someday, congratulating me for some verses I wrote in honor of Spring."

I believe, my son, our family is unjust with Mr. Peace; he seems a great lad to me, full of good sense.

And as for your cousin Pamela . . . Did you know, Eliacim, that your cousin Pamela had two lovers on the Continent?

Chapter 118: A Relatively Nice Cavalry Officer

I met him at the Fergussons's, Eliacim, and he was, from all appearances, officially nice, although I think that his niceness did not exceed a relative, although without any doubt, a very plausible, niceness. Tall, handsome, martial, he imitated, as no one else could, the croaking of frogs, the braying of donkeys, the chirping of little birds, the cawing of ravens, and the cackling of hens. The roar of a lion, the neighing of a horse, the lowing of a steer, especially on the sharp notes, the barking of a dog, the howling of a wolf, didn't come out too well.

The young officer performed to great effect some hand tricks which were difficult of execution, and he spoke Latin with a very funny accent; he knew a few rudiments of Swedish gymnastics and he danced marvelously. The marriageable girls quarreled over him. He's a charmer, they said, a real charmer.

The young cavalry officer took care, with excessive indulgence, of his old, paralytic mother, a poor lady who used to wet her bed, and used to edit the prayers with which the poor children of her neighborhood begged the help of God.

Looking at him very carefully, one could make out behind his bleached, fixed mask of niceness, a niceness praised by all, an intelligent and doleful sediment of bitterness.

You, Eliacim, since you were so sensible, pardon me, perhaps would not have guessed all by yourself, what I'm telling you now. But for that I would have been at your side, without leaving you, to explain it to you.

After the party at the Fergussons, Eliacim, I met the young officer again a few times. I saw him in the most unusual places, in the park, throwing bread crumbs to the birds, at the bus stop staring at a bewildered girl, in the post office, buying some air mail stamps, at the home of some mutual friends, displaying his sure abilities, and he always seemed to me deeply and bashfully heartbroken.

His jokes, Eliacim, although varied and almost always funny, used to have a remote double meaning behind which hunger could be seen. I don't know if I may be doing too much honor to the young and relatively nice cavalry officer, Eliacim, when I imagine him so beautifully unfortunate, but what is certain, my son, is that your mother, when she looked in his face, saw his spirit sort of shrivel up.

Fortunately, I haven't seen the young officer for some time now. Perhaps they've sent him out of the Isles. Perhaps, also, his mother has died and he doesn't feel obliged to be nice to people.

Chapter 119: Queen Anne Style

It's comfortable and gentle, Eliacim, with a solid, elegant line suited for use in families of a well-cemented position.

I would have liked to be a Queen Anne woman, Eliacim, a very fertile woman, not at all delicate, or so delicate, perhaps, that I could seem like a stony pyramid, and to have been the mother of many children whom I would not have loved at all, my dear, because all of my affection would have continued to be centered on you, but by whom I would be adored, almost with envy, from their Queen Anne childhoods up, even with certain adulterations.

I'm assaulted by the idea, which I wouldn't like to think too much about, so as not to tire myself out or make myself sad, of whether you would have been able to withstand the fierce dashing of the waves of fatality, the fierce attack of the sea, had I been a Queen Anne woman, strong as the Norman women. I don't want to insist on this point, for it would drive me crazy.

Chapter 120: River Navigation

1.

The broad, flat river boats, Eliacim, on the gentle and traitorous navigable rivers, sail with the current, decked out with their little flags in loud colors, exhaling polkas and military marches which reach the shore somewhat wet, whence they are greeted, with their dirty handkerchiefs, by the children of the public schools.

River navigation, my son, has a rare relationship with the most treacherous criminality; and a river, Eliacim, is always a little bit the memory of a horrible crime, of a crime committed on the little girl with swollen features who was strolling darkly through the narrowest and most lonely streets of the city.

The flat, keelless river boats, Eliaciam, on the calm, poisonous navigable rivers, sail against the current, with their bare masts and tall smoke stacks, dressed ordinarily, panting inhalations and expirations which don't reach the shore, that black-green shore whence no one manufactures smiles to tell them, "Goodbye, we wish you a pleasant voyage."

2.

Oh, my son! Whole squadrons of river boats sail through my veins—I don't know if they're still sailing—not elegant at all, certainly, not marine at all either; but they fulfill their duties almost shamefully, as the happy, ragged poor who were once rich beg alms, and they take me and carry me, up and down from nightmare to nightmare, from dying illusion to dying illusion, from fright to fright, to prevent my remaining asleep forever as at times I think is no longer my desire.

And on the prow of all those river boats, Eliacim, your

eyes are painted, with no longer any expression, just like the tired eyes of the stars.

I'm not telling you this so as to add more sadness to your sadness, my son. Nor am I saying it to pretend to be an abandoned mother.

3.

On that river boat which was named, like a harborside inn, "The Sea Gull which Speaks French Sweetly," a terrible thing happened to me, Eliacim, a thing which makes my hair stand on end. The truth is that I couldn't avoid it, but when I noticed that I had smothered it against my lap, my dear, I threw it over the rail, taking advantage of a moment in which no one was watching me. I can't go on telling you about it, Eliacim, because its begging eyes, those eyes which, careless woman that I am, I forgot to close, perhaps through lack of experience, pierce my eyes insistently.

Later, as time passed, I gave less and less importance to the event. Even though it had it, Eliacim, it had it.

4.

On holidays, the skippers give their river boats an extra ration, which consists of a dense and nutritious purée of corn flour with little pieces of fried bacon. On the river boats, on holidays, an unexpected sheen is born in their bellies, an unimaginable luster, and with their backbones more erect, Eliacim, they resemble young beasts which want to be sold at the fair, perhaps to change masters.

5.

After considerable study of the customs and traditions of river navigation, dear Eliacim, I am saddened by the idea that there is still a great deal that remains to be learned.

The boats, like soup tureens of the rivers like soup, my son, of the rivers which smell like the sap of sweet old forest trees, jealously guard, just as careful porcelain manufacturers, their secrets, the secrets that they have continued to inherit, generation after generation, since ancient times. And the children of the public schools, Eliacim, and I, who are now the only astonished spectators of river navigation, smile at them supplicatingly, on seeing them pass, so as to try to earn their sympathy. Even though, my son, I don't know to what point we'll be able to achieve it.

Chapter 121: Decisive Steps

You said: Tomorrow I'm going to take a decisive step in my life. And then you came home with a rouge stain on your shirt collar.

No, my son, let's not play so dangerously with words. That, Eliacim, that which occurred to you, was almost never much more than a not too decisive step. Decisive steps, my son, leave no trace: the pact with the devil is as aseptic as a well-equipped operating room.

Chapter 122: Oil Lamps

The era of oil lamps was nicer, Eliacim. Oil lamps were classified in three large groups: zoo lamps, herbal lamps, and sky lamps. The zoo lamps were decked out in butterflies, gazelles, fish. The herbal lamps showed tea roses, ferns, sweet peas. The sky lamps illuminated Cassiopeia, Aldebaran, Andromeda. You, had you known the oil lamp era, would have preferred to have on your night table, to read Sir Walter Scott by, a sky oil lamp, an oil lamp full of stars, constellations, and nebulae.

Yes, Eliacim, no doubt the oil lamp era was warmer and more merciful, the time in which an oil lamp of a good make and with carefully done animal, vegetable, or celestial decoration, could raise a family to the highest strata of society.

In your little grandmother's house, my son, at dusk, they always had this conversation around the oil lamp:

"It seems that the lamp lights up less. No, for heaven's sake! Perhaps the mantel is a little dirty. Albert! What are you saying? I'm sorry. It always takes a little time to reach its maximum brilliance at first. Certainly, it must be that it hasn't caught hold yet. Surely, surely. Yes, that's for sure. Careful, don't bump into the lamp. No, you don't have to bump into the lamp to talk," etc., ad infinitum.

(The characters were five, my son, and the phrases I've just mentioned might have been spoken by any one of us.)

Believe me, Eliacim, the era of the oil lamps was more protective, more homey. Did I tell you already that there were three classes of oil lamps: zoo lamps, herbal lamps, and sky lamps? Yes, I think I remember, yes, that I've already told you.

Chapter 123: On Desert Sands

On the sands of the desert, Eliacim, shine the clean and calcified bones of the most diverse origins: bones of camels, dromedaries, and horses, bones of Berber traders and Tuareg warriors, bones of lions, hyenas, and gazelles, bones of explorers, tourists, and missionaries, bones of the skull, coccyx, and extremities. On the sands of the desert, my son, is displayed a large selection of bones of the most various origins.

On the sands of the desert, Eliacim, I would have loved you impudently, bravely, as I never dared to love you in our city, more through fear, be sure of it, of the walls which sheltered us and the air which we breathed than of the people who could have watched us and even photographed us to our scorn and pride.

On the sands of the desert, my dearest, we women turn into insatiable and devasting hurricane winds, fierce wind-storms capable of leveling mountains and of burying cities. That is why it is forbidden, in the laws of some countries, for women to appear in the desert with the same freedom as we can at a high balustrade.

On the sands of the desert, Eliacim, our steps squeak as if we were walking on a bed of dry shameful desires, of sterile desires which we would dare to confess only at the moment of death.

But on the sands of the desert, Eliacim, among the tibias and fibulas which married in great luxury, and disappeared without a trace, we could still see each other, without any-one succeeding in finding out, and give each other our can-teens to drink from.

Chapter 124: The Problem of the Colored Peoples

The problem of the colored peoples bothers only the whites. And, today, Eliacim, we have things in hand, but tomorrow, who knows what will happen tomorrow?

Yes, it's better, doubtless, for the colored peoples to exist and even prosper, better that there be Negroes, yellow-skinned, olive-skinned and also red-skinned men with poetical hunter's names.

If the colored peoples disappeared suddenly, Eliacim, who would fill the immense vacuum which they would leave in the world?

Among the colored peoples, it's possible that a parallel worry does not exist, my son, because the colored peoples, by dint of listening to us, realized in time that the best and most relaxed thing was to let us have our way.

And this idea, Eliacim, is something which upsets the white man, unhinges us and leads us along the road of sorrow.

Chapter 125: A Great Show

Since it had been announced with all due ceremony, Eliacim, you put on your dinner jacket and went to the theater, quickly and full of hope.

The theater, my son, was animated that night as never before. Miss Fiore achieved what very few women any longer achieve: men gave her expensive bouquets of flowers, even after having taken care to disappear with a bullet in their temple.

In the seat next to you, Eliacim, was seated, by chance, the suicide in row eleven, that young banker who couldn't resign himself to waiting, to giving an example of patience until his turn, or let's say, his hour came, in the hard heart of Miss Fiore.

I, Eliacim, spent one whole day trying to get the blood

stains out of your clothes, but my heart filled with illusion knowing that you had come through it so well.

It was a great show, an unforgettable show! you told me, thinking perhaps, that you would have many years of life ahead of you to remember it always.

Chapter 126: Archery

Archery is nobler, Eliacim, in the sense of more aristocratic, more useless, perhaps also more gallant, than shooting a slingshot. Slingshooting is more amusing, more in accord with our hobbies, my son; but you know that we cannot always do that which pleases us.

The figure of the archer has, Eliacim, a rhythmical elegance which is not achieved by the figure of the slingshooter. Ancient painters, when they wanted to show some well-proportioned features, a prince, a young cardinal, a victorious captain, always tried to copy, line by line, the shape of an archer. On the other hand, when they wanted to fix on the canvas a plebeian face, a conquistador, a saint, a workman, they looked for their model among the herd of slingshooters.

Archery, Eliacim, educates the will, and quiets the trees of the nerves. Among the Greek children, my son, in the time of the patricians, many years ago, but not many miles from where you are, it was the custom to train for politics and high enterprises, by making their first combat with the bow. Remember, Eliacim, that the Greek world, according to authorities on the subject, was a model of deliberate political maturity.

I never got (it's also certain that I never tried to) you to conceive, my dear, a real fondness for archery. And now, I think, Eliacim, that I would have been very pleased to know that you were a consummate archer, and to be able to tell that to my friends and relatives, as if I didn't give it too much importance.

Chapter 127: The Wax Museum

In our city, Eliacim, I miss a wax museum, a well-equipped museum, with heating and indirect lighting, in which we could see, in their own environments, Nero, Torquemada, Marat, Jack, Landru, the modern Dr. Petiot, and all the great murderers of humanity.

Wax museums are, Eliacim, highly educational for youth, and for the ruling class, and their establishment ought, in my opinion, to be furthered by the public authorities.

In the absence of taxidermy, my son, which could depict famous people for us in a more lifelike way, wax does very well, since it can at least depict famous people for us in a more deathlike way.

Strolling among the showcases, as big as bedrooms, of the wax museum, Eliacim, I think I'd be happy being able to take in, with my eyes and at one stroke, all the specters that terrorized people of their time, all the black shadows which today are displayed, like stuffed birds, for our most decorous voracity.

I regret never having spoken to you, when I could have done it with more immediate efficacy, of my fondness for wax museums, for jails, or watering places, where we shut up some wax beards and some glass eyes, which we baptize according to our preferences.

We would have had a good time, you and I, Eliacim, visiting our friends, the greatest murderers of humanity, and sticking out our tongues at them, well protected by the regulations. Don't you agree?

Chapter 128: Chess

The most violent hatreds, my dearest, the deepest abysses of hate, separate erudite men, musicians, and chess players.

Chess, Eliacim, is a hateful game that has had a good press, an apology for treason which has dressed itself in the innocuous, white lambskin of a pastime.

When you and I used to play chess, and as if carelessly, I won one game after another, Eliacim, sinister sparks appeared in your look, sparks which your smile could not extinguish, while the black, sick raven of revenge stood in your throat with one wing resting on your palate, the mortuary bird which weighs hearts down.

Yes, Eliacim, yes. You were too much involved in the problem to be able to see it with even a minimum of calm, with that calm which would have been, let it be said now since the occasion presents itself, so advantageous.

The planet where the rooks, bishops and knights developed in their preordained orbits, my son, is a dead heavenly body on which will never grow the humble blade of grass on which we lean our aching, scourged flesh, when it can't be helped.

Chess, Eliacim, is a game for astigmatic souls, something which we ought to separate from ourselves like a bitter cup. Only when we do this, Eliacim, and man regains the liberty which permits him to move the pieces as he wishes, will we be able to confront, without too much oppression, this brief life which escapes from us like a wheel rolling downhill.

Chapter 129: Tobacco

When you smoked your first cigarette (I mean, naturally, your first permitted cigarette) and blew, as if to annihilate me with your elegance, a large mouthful of smoke through your nose, I was on the point of bursting out crying disconsolately, Eliacim, like a woman very much in love with her husband who received over the telephone the news that she had suddenly become a widow.

Tobacco, my son, is good for the health, although at times it is bad for the health. If one could give a cigarette to the orphans and the needy in time, Eliacim, there would be from then on, many fewer people classified as orphans or needy to receive welfare. But no one has taken seriously this strategic distribution of cigarettes, and so things go on as they do.

Among all the tobacco which I know of, my son, none has the firm curative virtues of Havana tobacco, that aromatic combustible, capable of reviving lost causes or of setting straight and leading aimless hearts along the right road. If I had great persuasive force, Eliacim, if I were a great political or religious orator, an effective political agitator or religious apostle with a solid clientele, I would undertake a crusade on behalf of Havana tobacco, under the slogan: "Don't let them burn you; burn!"

But, Eliacim, since I know my own limitations, I am satisfied with smoking from time to time a cigar which lends me a great confidence in myself, and which returns to me, or I imagine it returns to me, very many needlessly lost energies.

Yes, Eliacim, with that old practice of one puff for me and one for you, I spend my lonely evenings with a certain resignation, with all of the slight joy of which I now feel myself capable.

When you smoked your first cigarette (now you know what kind of first cigarette I'm referring to), and spoke a few brief words before exhaling the smoke, with an impertinently gracious gesture, through your nose, I almost burst out crying enthusiastically, like a repentant sinner.

Chapter 130: Your Training Voyage

The itinerary of your training voyage, Eliacim, could have filled you with happiness. What a great pleasure for me to know that you were so happy on the distant seas which at first seemed so favorable for you, and ended up by acting so badly toward you and toward me!

Gibraltar. I bought myself a guitar, a pair of banderillas (the weapons with which bullfighters defend themselves against the fierce attack of the bull) and a bottle of real Sherry wine. The makers of Sherry wines are very solvent, the Mackenzies, Gordons, Williams, Sandemans, Spencers, Osbornes, Terrys; Mr. Gonzalez is also very well known.

Algiers. I bought myself some babouches, a kif pipe, and a copper tray which I think you will like. It is very pretty here; the houses are all white and some women have their faces covered.

Naples. I have bought some bone amulets which guard against shipwrecks, and a collection of postal cards. Here there are many shoeshine boys and the hairdressers are very nice, although somewhat confused about the bills.

Alexandria. I have bought a porcelain tea set. When I got on board I saw that on the teapot in tiny letters it says "Made in Germany."

Port Said. I have bought some opera glasses which are also perhaps German.

Colombo. I bought a pearl necklace to give you when I return home. The second mate laughed a lot when I told him about it and he explained to me that these pearls are "Made in Japan."

Singapore. I bought some novels by Vicki Baum. At first sight, not being very accustomed to it, it is not easy to distinguish between the Chinese, the Indochinese, and the Malayans.

Manila. I bought a Manila shawl and a little ivory box. I don't want to ask, but I heard that they are also Japanese.

Hong-Kong. I bought a copy of *The Times*.

The list of your purchases, my son, would be a never-ending tale, it would be the complete itinerary of your training voyage, your long and happy training voyage.

And now I see the list of your purchases, Eliacim; the collection of postal cards which you kept sending me, like a dutiful son, from all over the world, with a cold sensation of strangeness. It is very difficult for me to think, Eliacim, that these cards were addressed to me, from the farthest corners of the world, precisely by you, my dear.

Chapter 131: The Softest Meadows

On the softest meadows, Eliacim, on the green meadows which resemble stretches of sweet paradise, my son, the deer graze, full of meekness, and the members of the House of Lords play golf.

Some mornings it occurs to me to think, Eliacim, that the deer are the happiest animals of all, happier even than man, than the members of the House of Lords, who also have their worries, though none too great.

If, before being born, we were given the choice of the fate we were to have, Eliacim, I would choose, with my eyes closed, to be a timid deer in the meadows, a gentle deer in the most tender and delicate meadows.

Because in the meadows, my dear, the gleam of the hand of God still shines from time to time, that merciful hope which appears as green grass, as a graceful blade which lives silently, intensely, its very solid and minimal satisfaction.

Over the softest meadows, Eliacim, flies that pure feeling the same color as the air, which I can't manage to have toward you.

Chapter 132: The Bird Cage

I.

In a huge bird cage, Eliacim, in an immense cage in which the birds would keep for ages the joy of knowing themselves to be captives, I would keep your tiny heart until it sprouted wings the intimate color of the apple blossom.

If we could get the birds, Eliacim, when your heart began to fly like a bird, to feed on your own heart, cutting its wings with their beaks and crushing it like a tender piece of fruit, we could feel, my dear, firmer and more lasting, stonier and more immutable in our own weak convictions.

But the shiny birds in the bird cage, Eliacim, the birds who sing, from morning to night, for no reason (let's grant them that much), feed only on fresh hearts, on healthy hearts, on beating hearts disguised, just like happy masks, by bliss.

2.

Your heart, my dear, became the colors of the hoarse sound of the sea, Eliacim, and is no longer good for bird food.

3.

But listen to what I am telling you, my son, if only so that I may feel a breath of a happy breeze airing out my soul: if no one could find out, I would take the hearts from all the boys your age, Eliacim. And over the huge mountain of hearts, Eliacim, I would hang a great golden bird cage full of spiders.

Chapter 133: Narrow-Waisted Mistress Wanted

You placed, Eliacim, in the proper section, an advertisement which filled me with pain: "Narrow-Waisted Mistress Wanted."

Why, my dear, such cruel precision? Your mother, Eliacim, for many years had a narrow waist admired by everybody, perhaps you can still remember it. But the time of

adversity came, my son, and your mother, who had to neg-
lect almost everything, lost, almost without realizing it, her
narrow waist, that narrow waist admired by everybody
which you, perhaps, may still remember.

Even without a narrow waist, Eliacim, a woman can make
a man very happy, so happy that he may not come to know
in a strict sense, which are really the narrow waists and
which the wide waists.

I was filled with a bitter pain, Eliacim, by your brief and
inconsiderate advertisement. I also would have preferred to
have a son who never left me.

Why don't you whisper in my ear six or eight words
which can erase the bad effect your advertisement had on
me?

Chapter 134: Some Immense, Virtuous Lips

Your lips, my dear, were not immense and virtuous, they
were polite and normal-sized. But had they been immense
and virtuous, Eliacim, immense and virtuous like fire, for
example, I would not have dared to look at them with the
audacity with which at times, very few times of course! I
dared to.

(Think that a mother, my dear, almost always has the
right to look, at any hour of the day and with whatever
gesture she pleases, at the lips of her only son.)

But your lips, Eliacim, with the passage of time, would
have come to be immense and virtuous like those I liked,
immense and virtuous as I need them and as you, probably,
had you had them, would have needed so as not to die, so as
not to cheat me.

I'm terrified by the thought that your lips, my dear, have

decomposed already and are swimming in thousands and thousands of tiny fragments, through the cold wilderness of the mermaids, those insatiable ghosts with immense and virtuous lips, immense and wisely virtuous lips.

There are things which I don't feel strong enough to think about.

Chapter 135: Yes

It's a beautiful hiss, Eliacim, which we usually let escape with an ignorant indifference, without hurrying to seize it. To hear you pronounce it, Eliacim, I asked you the most varied and foreseeable things: have you bathed? is it daytime? are you going out? do you want a cup of tea? are you happy?

I never failed with you, my dear, because I never asked you a single word about which I had the slightest doubt of your reply. Women, Eliacim, when we no longer need it for anything, feel a rare instinct come alive in our hearts, a hot and heavy instinct like the doorway of a lit oven.

Yes, Eliacim, is always a pleasant breath of hope.

Chapter 136: The White Rocks Beaten by the Sea

The youngest suicides, my dear, those whose heads are organized like those of the French novelists, dream at night of lovers' walks among the white rocks beaten by the sea.

Theirs are usually walks which begin badly only to end

well, the opposite of the dreams of virtuous girls, those who do not permit the occasion to arise of feeling themselves loved on the white rocks beaten by the sea.

The dreams of the youngest suicides, Eliacim, are cruelly clear and precise and the man who kisses them, the white rock, the roaring sea, surges, precise and vivid, with a reality which fills their hearts with grief.

The man who kisses them, Eliacim, whose hands are red with blood, my dear, usually speaks to them with familiarity and a lack of respect.

"Meg, pull out your hair and throw it up high, so the wind will carry it away!"

Meg, doing herself terrible harm, pulls out her hair and throws it up high so that the wind may carry it away.

"Betsy, put out your eyes and drop them on the ground, and take care that they do not break, so that the ants may eat them!"

Betsy, trembling with pain, puts out her eyes and drops them on the ground, and takes care that they do not break, so that the voracious, diligent ants may eat them up.

"Nancy, kiss me!"

Nancy kisses him.

The white rock, Eliacim, whose old age is green with blood, my dear, usually speaks to them with a familiar ferocity.

"Bel, beat your breasts with a stone, put them in your hand, and blow on them strongly, so that I will see them fly!"

Bel, crying disconsolately, beats her breasts with a stone, puts them in her hand, blows on them with all her strength, so that the white rock can see them fly.

"Molly, bite off your tongue and spit it out so that it will wave in the wind like a flag!"

Molly, full of loathing, a pleasant and gentle loathing like the scorn of a child, bites off her tongue, and spits it out, so that it can wave in the thin wind like a torn flag.

"Jinny, kiss me!"

Jinny, on her knees, kisses the white rock.

The roaring sea, Eliacim, whose water is gray with blood, my dear, usually speaks to them with a familiar coldness, like a father pretending to be offended.

"Kitty, fall!"

And Kitty falls.

"Fan, fall!"

And Fan falls.

"Maudlin, fall!"

And Maudlin, closing her eyes, falls.

Yes, Eliacim, the youngest suicides, those who have their heads as well designed as those of the French poets, dream, on the most humid and receptive evenings, about long, impossible lovers' walks over the white rocks beaten by the sea.

It's not so bad if theirs are usually walks which end with an expected finale, like good plays.

Chapter 137: Pen Drawings

With various little bottles of colored ink, Eliacim, and various pens so that the inks do not mix and the colors do not get muddy, one can make pretty pictures, a boat, a flower, a

Dutch peasant woman, two or three trees, a beggar, a swan swimming among red, yellow, and blue flowers.

When you were a child, Eliacim, still a very small boy, your father (God rest his soul) gave you some colored pencils which you took with a sullen gesture because what you wanted, my son, was to draw with a pen the most tender and fleeting objects, a sunken ship, a dead flower, a Malayan peasant girl, two or three trees under the snow, a beggar who was tired of walking, a swan.

Since you were so small, Eliacim, you still hadn't lost the virtue of ignoring almost all the impossibilities.

Pen drawings, Eliacim, are usually the work of very experienced artists, veterans.

Chapter 138: Heresies

Heresies, my son, are like coins, which, besides having two sides, always presuppose an accepted value.

Don't force me to explain too much what I prefer to leave vaguely veiled.

Chapter 139: Respiratory Gymnastics

It is healthy, so I've heard, to do some respiratory gymnastics exercises when you get up. The lungs stretch and are toned up, the blood is refreshed, and the heart jumps for joy at getting it so fresh, so lusty, so recently washed.

I don't know all that there might be in this of truth or

falsity, Eliacim. What I do remember is that, when they put that idea in your head about respiratory gymnastics, you spent a few days talking to yourself, like a sleepwalker, and scolding me for everything.

"Are you ill, my son?"

"No, I'm fine, perfectly fine, why?"

"Nothing, nothing."

You were very susceptible and anything infuriated you and exasperated you.

"Why do you ask me if I'm ill? Do you think I'm ill? I have a right to know how you think I am, whether well or ill: I have an absolute right to know!"

No, Eliacim, no; let's not exaggerate. You didn't have the right to know how I thought you were, whether well or ill; I always found you well, you know that. You were required to know that I always found you well. What unhappiness you gave me during that happy time of respiratory gymnastics, my son!

Chapter 140: Still Lifes

Still life painters, Eliacim, differ very little; perhaps the fact is that the still life is something which in itself has very little variety, I don't know.

Still life painters, Eliacim, are usually happy and they sing, like the morgue keepers, my dear, who sing tender melodies among the dead, and kiss on their mouths, with their taste of the dead, the plump cooks of the neighborhood, the handsome and buxom cooks, full of life, that there are in the neighborhood, who are deceiving their sweethearts, the fruiterer or the carpenter, who do not smell or taste of death, with the morgue keeper, who has the breath of the dead hidden in his wisdom tooth.

Still life painters, Eliacim, paint with a mask so as to pass unrecognized.

But I, dearest son, know several who could not pretend. If I had the chance, I would show them to you when they go through the streets taking their little children to school. The little children of still life painters have a great propensity for dying by being run over by a taxi or a bus.

Chapter 141: Leisure

Leisure is beneficial, my son; leisure is the pleasant gift of the gods, a benevolent blessing of the gods. I think, Eliacim, that if one could store up leisure, if one could manufacture and market it as happens with other products, one could lend a great service to man.

Men with leisure, my son, men who harbor in their spirits such peace that nothing impels them to work, are the very image of the highest moral perfection.

If you had become a man, Eliacim, a mature man and father, perhaps you would have understood more easily that what I am telling you is as clear as day. I know very well that at your age, Eliacim, no one should expect anything but guesswork, hunches, presentiments. Experience is a fruit which matures more slowly, and leisure, my son, is a difficult and long experience.

In your lengthy submarine leisure, Eliacim, do you sometimes remember me?

In your lengthy submarine leisure, my dear, don't you

have a presentiment, don't you intuit, don't you guess that we could have been briefly and intensely happy at the moment in which our leisures, yours still so tender, coincided like the moon and the sun in an eclipse, one on top of the other?

Chapter 142: The Strangest and Healthiest Women

The strangest and healthiest women, Eliacim, are usually found among the middle class, perhaps because it is also the most numerous and innocuous.

The strangest and healthiest women, my dear, make themselves up like gentle, meek cattle, so as to be better able to pass unnoticed. Also, Eliacim, in order to defend themselves better in the daily struggle against misery.

The strangest and healthiest women, Eliacim, usually have a scorpion's nest in their bosoms, a crowd of scorpions lashing them on their high, powerful breast.

It gives me great peace, my son, a great interior calm, to know that you are far away from these strange and healthy women forever, the strangest and healthiest women that anyone could ever conceive of.

Chapter 143: I Cannot Manage to Ignore

So many are the things, my son, which I cannot manage to ignore, that sometimes, amid bitter tears, I would gladly trade myself for anything which could feel detached, ignorant of all these things to which I, Eliacim, what a curse! can never feel myself alien.

I cannot manage to ignore, my son, the time which passes, the rain which falls, the tea which I drink, the man I pass on the street, the dog, stiff with cold, which scratches the door of the house, your memory. And what I would wish, my dear, I swear it, would be not to have so many, many things torturing me, so many, many things reminding me each instant that I cannot manage to ignore them and live freely.

Things, Eliacim, would show nobler feelings by disappearing forever, like a tear which falls into the sea.

Chapter 144: Dirty Snow

I love dirty snow, Eliacim, snow trodden by people whose names I don't know, snow which becomes the color of hands which struggle to satisfy their hunger and which suddenly, without knowing how, find themselves caressing a belly as smooth as an apple, an exploding belly.

On this sweetly dirty snow, my son, I would let myself die abandoned, just like an abandoned child, with my eyes staring at some ordinary object being covered little by little by the new fallen snow, like an implacable tide.

And on this carnally dirty snow, Eliacim, I do not think death would bother me. Death is something which weighs on others' shoulders, on the shoulders which any mother, in a moment of bewilderment, could have made.

I love the dirty snow, Eliacim, the snow given to all the men of the city.

Chapter 145: That Accursed Air Which Sleeps among the Houses

That accursed air which sleeps among the houses is found in the place where the filthiest and mangiest cats make love, where the musicians who became tubercular from blowing the trumpet smother, where fish heads rot, where the masturbating children hide, where the commercial traveler urinates, where the rat rubescent with the plague suckles her young, where the most cautious thieves meet, where the mothers of families prostitute themselves, where the most abject cold is felt, where no one remembers to smile.

That accursed air which sleeps among the houses, Eliacim, engenders at times the highest thoughts of charity; it sometimes illuminates unsuspected and gallant thoughts of hope, clear and arrogant, like thunder.

I don't know why it is, my son, but in the place where that accursed air sleeps among the houses, at times, you can also hear human words in the mouths of sick cats in love, or you can hear a flute played with a tinge of feeling and mystery, or you can make out dead sea-breams and hakes which look like young girls, or you know that a child is praying without opening his lips, or a commercial traveler who was left without goods is dying of fatigue, or that the white rat with the plague is cured by a miracle, or that the most daring thieves decide not to steal anymore, or the mothers of families toil to find a piece of hard bread under the stones, or that you can see in their flesh a warm flash of mercy, or someone remembers in time to put a smile on their face.

Everything is a question, son, of getting accustomed to breathing that accursed air which sleeps among the houses.

There are days when it would be impossible for me to forget it, impossible to live without it.

Chapter 146: Charms

You, Eliacim, had always been very fond of charms. Most of all the charms, Eliacim, you preferred those of bone, silver, wood, and iron, in that order; you disdained those of copper, and you couldn't stand those of putty at all. In this, as in everything, there are preferences, and sympathies, and hatreds and antipathies. It's something I won't go into.

Your charms, my son, had the most various applications, the most diverse employments. In your charm collection, Eliacim, there were charms to make people fall in love, charms to conjure up evil spirits, charms to bring rain, charms to cure illnesses, charms to drive away fire, charms to give happiness in childbirth, charms to preserve youth and beauty, charms to orient the compass properly for voyages, and charms to free one from shipwrecks. These, Eliacim, were the ones which gave us the least results, those which behaved most poorly and inconsiderately with us.

You were always a great fan of charms, my son, and I inherited your fondness along with your collection.

Sometimes, when I have nothing to do, I clean your charms one by one. I like to take good care of them.

Chapter 147: For Three Days I Loved the Farmer Tom Dickinson

Tuesday, the 7th

Tom Dickinson, my dear, is wonderful. Tom Dickinson is tall and strong, he knows how to mow hay and milk cows, shoe horses and prune rosebushes.

Tom Dickinson, Eliacim, sings some old Welsh songs, full of nostalgia, while drawing water from the well. Tom Dickinson has a beautiful baritone voice and teeth as white and sharp as a wolf's.

Tom Dickinson, dear, is saving to buy a tractor which will help him work his farm.

Wednesday, the 8th

Tom Dickinson's farm, my son, is rather small, but glistening, prosperous, and carefully looked after.

Tom Dickinson's farm, Eliacim, has green pastures, new stables, potato and oat fields where the morning wind plays.

Tom Dickinson's farm, my son, grows and lives around a comfortable house in which the fire burns all day and all night.

Thursday, the 9th

Tom Dickinson's house, my son, is two stories high; aside from the cellar and the loft: the cellar full of bottles of wine, the loft stuffed with threshed grain.

Tom Dickinson's house, Eliacim, is decorated with solid and simple furniture and some bright curtains in happy, lively colors.

Tom Dickinson's house, my son, saves all the light which enters its windows for Tom Dickinson.

Friday, the 10th

Tom Dickinson, my son, walks around in his house like a king, haughty like a king, more serene, and happier than a king.

Eliacim, for three days, Tuesday, Wednesday and Thursday of this week, I loved the farmer Tom Dickinson.

But I didn't want to tell him, my son, because I was afraid of doing wrong.

Chapter 148: The Drowned Man's Wallet

It was soft, Eliacim, and dull, the drowned man's wallet, with its keys, its faded family photograph, and its three pennies.

I got great consolation, at first, out of being able to touch the young drowned man of the wallet with my foot; but then it surprised me greatly to see that he wasn't smiling.

When the ambulance took the young drowned man away, Eliacim, the wallet remained, unnoticed, on the cold and wet stones of the jetty. I thought that a bad spot and, unnoticed, I picked it up and pressed it to my heart.

Now, Eliacim, since I found the drowned man's wallet, I sleep with it under my pillow and I feel relatively happier.

They must have done an autopsy on the young drowned man, as is customary with the young men the sea gives back. I say a short prayer for him every night. But I don't want to burn his wallet; I couldn't.

Chapter 149: A Valiant Cat

My friend, Martha MacCloy, the widow of Zoroaster MacCloy, that very funny vegetarian you knew, has a valiant cat, a gentleman cat, a cat in whom one of Richard the Lionheart's or of Charlemagne's captains is surely incarnate.

My friend Martha MacCloy's cat is tiger-striped and not very fat and he is no known breed, although he does have a pretty first name. My friend Martha MacCloy's cat is called Lucius Gamester. Do you like it?

Well, my son, Lucius Gamester, as I was saying, is a

valiant cat. The other day, just like that, I was visiting my friend Martha MacCloy, when we heard a tremendous commotion on the roof.

"Goodness," said my friend Martha MacCloy. "Now Lucius Gamester is settling some question of honor on the roof! It's unbearable, my friend, I assure you, always to have to put up with Lucius Gamester's gentlemanliness all day! I think that if he doesn't stop it he'll finally drive me crazy."

The valiant cat of my friend, Eliacim, disappeared the other day without leaving a trace. I think, although I didn't tell Martha MacCloy, that Lucius Gamester was an out-and-out gambler.

Chapter 150: Clay and Smoke

To play with clay, Eliacim, to get my hands and dress soiled with clay, is something which has come to corrupt me, my son, something for which I would be capable of doing anything.

I don't know, I don't know, but I think that playing with clay is something which is given only to very special spirits, people who have demonstrated their capacity to play with clay without swearing.

Clay, my son, that which is neither sea nor land, neither water nor earth, can be very dangerous if you don't approach it with all your remorse in tow and all your senses alert and on guard.

Of course, Eliacim, rest assured that it is something which cannot be left in everyone's hands.

Smoke, on the contrary, can be, Eliacim. Smoke is somewhat more democratic, and in order to handle it, no special training is needed. Smoke can be used without danger by everyone, including even the stupidest people. Smoke takes revenge at times and stains and soils our hearts; but these violent outbursts are fortunately very rare.

Smoke, my son, is like sleep, something you cannot grasp. If we could fill our pockets with smoke, Eliacim, and put it on the table like a coin, smoke would lose its charm.

Clay can be put on a table; the only thing is that it is not advisable.

Chapter 151: Dorothy

I have some bad news for you, Eliacim. Dorothy, sweet Dorothy, that obliging little girl of whom it was said that she would marry well, died in hospital. (I didn't like seeing her wrapped up in that sheet, which did nothing for her, that sheet which they might have taken the trouble to iron a little.)

Do you remember, Eliacim, how nervous you got the time that Dorothy, playing forfeits, asked you to kiss her with a little enthusiasm, but without passion? I laugh every time I remember.

Dorothy, a little before she died, asked me as a favor to come and visit her. Naturally I left for the hospital right away.

"How are you, Dorothy? I didn't know that you had been brought to hospital."

"Yes, I am in hospital because burials are more convenient from here. I am aware."

"Surely. But, Dorothy, child, you aren't going to die, you are strong enough to live for many years."

Dorothy smiled. "Yes, ma'am, I am going to die the day after tomorrow. I have almost no strength left. The little strength I have I don't think will last me more than two days."

"No, my woman. Put away those thoughts."

Dorothy smiled again. "What for?"

Dorothy was very beautiful, my son, I assure you. In two days, just as she had figured, she died.

I sent her some flowers which didn't arrive in time. In the hospital where Dorothy died, my son, burials are so convenient that the flowers never arrive in time.

Chapter 152: The Sad Schoolboy

The other day, I missed the chance to buy myself a sad schoolboy; they would have sold him to me cheap. His parents sought to leave him in good hands for only one pound and six shillings. I enjoyed haggling over the price a little, because the sad schoolboy first of all needed shoes and then needed to be dressed from head to toe, but a woman spoke up first and carried him off by the hand.

The sad schoolboy, when his mistress carried him off by the hand, didn't turn his head. You can see that he wasn't overly interested in what he was leaving behind.

I, my son, was curious, and hastened to catch up with him. The sad schoolboy was no sadder than usual; that's not even true: he was happier. The sad schoolboy was walking woodenly, looking at the ground and running his hand along the wall.

The woman who had bought him, although harsh in appearance, seemed well intentioned and, from time to time, she rapped the sad schoolboy, not very hard, on the head. The sad schoolboy received the blow on his carrot-colored hair, and neither shrugged, nor flinched, nor dodged, nor straightened up. Perhaps he didn't even notice.

The mistress of the sad schoolboy, my son, when they passed a sweets shop bought a mint caramel, cut it more or less in half, and gave the sad schoolboy his share, the smaller piece: she sucked the other a little and then put it in her purse, wrapped in tissue paper. One could see at once, Eliacim, that the mistress of the sad schoolboy was a very careful lady.

I, my son, followed the sad schoolboy and his mistress for a long while, since I had nothing better to do.

At a grocer's, the sad schoolboy was bought three biscuits. The sad schoolboy ate two and put the third in his pants' pocket.

The sad schoolboy's pants, Eliacim, were a deep mine of unimaginable treasures, of endless riches which the sad schoolboy, my son, tempered with the warmth of his groin and caressed on the sly when he had the slightest chance of not being seen.

I can never regret enough, my dear, having allowed the chance of owning the sad schoolboy to slip by. In our home, Eliacim, the sad schoolboy would have been able to play the lively role of a cornet.

I am only consoled by the idea, my son, that the sad schoolboy, as time went on, would get to tear the heart out of the lady who bought him. Probably, the sad schoolboy would commit his evil deed with horrible, startling guffaws.

Chapter 153: Background Music

There is an entire technique, Eliacim, a technique which certainly cannot be very difficult at all, of background music. Musicians who specialize in this sort of music, my son, usually have the crevices of their head clouded by a warm, translucent mist which raises their temperature and shuts off their capacity for admitting light in proportion to the emotional intensity of the situation.

They place a manometer on their adrenal glands and they work automatically, like electric refrigerators. It couldn't be any easier.

Chapter 154: The Happiness Shirt

In an old Persian story, Eliacim, you will recall, there was a man, perhaps he was a beggar, I couldn't tell you exactly, who was very happy because he didn't have a shirt.

With me, my son, exactly the opposite happens. I, in order to be happy, need to wear a certain item, in a given color, in a proper and well-known shape, of a certain, definite quality.

(Naturally, my son, your mother has not been referring just now to a shirt, an item which woman threw overboard many years ago. Could you guess, Eliacim, you, since you're now a man, what sort of article I am alluding to? I will give you another hint which may help orient you: at this moment I feel feverish, although also relaxed.)

Chapter 155: The Stuffed Deer

1.

With his gentle, with his unsettling glass eyes, my dear, the stuffed deer stares fixedly at me from the wall. The last time you left home, Eliacim, you said goodbye, and even with a certain amount of emotion, to our stuffed deer, who also stared at you fixedly, with his placid, with his sinning glass eyes, from the wall.

There were moments, when I was left alone after your departure, when I thought that the stuffed deer was going to say some consoling word to me, some kind condescending word. But the stuffed deer, Eliacim, limited himself to looking at me without blinking, as if at a very strange object, with his mysterious crystal eyes.

2.

With his caramel horns, Eliacim, with his sweet, offensive horns, my son, the stuffed deer threatened me every morning. The last time that I dusted him, Eliacim, with my little feather duster and the same care as always, I found his familiar, disgraceful horns, my darling, warmer than usual, somewhat more, how shall I say? receptive and firm.

Since then I haven't dusted him again with my little duster; don't forget, Eliacim, that I am living absolutely alone.

3.

With his sad and resigned air, Eliacim, the deer who looks at me and threatens me from the wall, and this is the truth, makes good company. He still doesn't look at me, nor speak to me, nor smile at me, surely, but I think that all that will change.

You can't get stuffed deer, Eliacim, to react just like that.

Chapter 156: Blank Paper

Everything we know, Eliacim, can be written on a not very large piece of blank paper. Drawing on the paper, with care to outline the strokes, the letters of the alphabet, and making the possible combinations with them, my son, one would get to put together two or three plays of Shakespeare and even of someone else. The bad thing about it is that it would take a long time.

The great literary works of the future, Eliacim, are asleep in blank paper, the great literary works which are still to be written. Sometimes I feel tempted to confront the blank paper, and begin to put down letters, one after another, to see what comes out. There are some who say that Latin was invented in a similar way; I don't know.

Chapter 157: The Odors Which Arouse Our Bad Instincts

The odors which arouse our bad instincts, Eliacim, the odors which arouse the vilest and most delicate instincts, my son, are usually, frequently, the best odors, officially the best odors: rose, jasmine, violet.

When you were a boy, Eliacim, I always perfumed you with rose, with jasmine, or with violet, according to what I wished to imagine I would get from you. I used rose to make you look at me indecently; jasmine to disguise you as a spiteful lover; violet so as never to know that you would deny yourself, with such stubborn insistence, at the most incorruptible smiles of your mother.

The odors which arouse our bad instincts, Eliacim, are dissolved in the world, floating over the world, awaiting whoever wants to smell them.

The men and women who have smelled a lot, my son, the odors which arouse our bad instincts, usually possess a great peace, like a little bird, poised in their glance.

Chapter 158: League of Acid-Resistant Bacilli

The IInd Assembly of the LARB (League of Acid-Resistant Bacilli) which met, some time ago, in Hamburg, reached some curious conclusions. You were the discoverer, and the discovery filled you with glory and pride. I think that you discovered it by pure chance; pardon me, Eliacim; I don't think of you as having a privileged brain, but I do, relatively, as a good son.

The plan conceived by the LARB for the extermination of the human race is well designed in general. Some few mistakes can be rectified at any time, while under way.

The Lucky Koch bacillus, a young Caucasian cultivated in Boston, placed the question well and didn't permit any digressions or loss of time. In reality, the young Lucky Koch is a first-class parliamentarian and his presence was exemplary and efficient.

In this IInd Assembly, only one question was dealt with: "The extermination of the human species, a necessary step toward the conquest of power."

The amendments which were presented by those assembled who thought it more convenient to begin with bovine cattle, were quickly rejected. Observe, my son, that the lack of consistency usually leads to nothing good.

Herr Augustus Friedenberg, in whose lungs the sessions of the LARB were being held, wished to end the Assembly, and had recourse to the rhymiphone, streptomycin, and pneumothorax. Herr Augustus Friedenberg had slight success because the LARB, like all persecuted organizations, drew strength from weakness and approved its conclusions in one continuous session. In reality, Herr Augustus Friedenberg, as always happens, was right to some extent. Why, Herr Augustus Friedenberg asked himself, must my lungs be the permanent headquarters of the LARB? Let them go to Liverpool, which doesn't have a bad climate either. Although Herr Augustus, my son, as I told you, was not wrong, no one paid him any mind. Take note of this, Eliacim. (Before I forget; that bill for coiled paper ribbons which I mentioned to you—do you remember? which seemed a little excessive to me—I've already paid it. I would never have done it, but there were reasons which I have no reason for making known to you.)

The human race, according to LARB, is divided, for extermination purposes, into three groups: A, B, and C. In A belong those persons whom it is best to eliminate as soon as possible (doctors, chemists, philanthropists, etc.); in B, the human beings whose destruction must not be put off if propitious circumstances present themselves (pharmacists, architects, etc.); and in C, those others who, for different reasons, had better be saved until the end (politicians, strategists, arms makers, etc.) The lists have no names as you can see, but are classified according to occupation or activity.

I enjoy repeating what you already know, Eliacim, what you yourself made known to me, because, although I insist that I am not very sure that the discovery is yours, it is always salutary, I think, for one to pretend, even if she doesn't feel herself, to be the mother of a genius.

Group A is made up of . . .

Chapter 159: The Broken Fountain

That broken fountain in the garden, my son, when winter came and snow fell on it, sang with its quietest voice, a voice like that of newly married fireflies, a few thin and amorous laments which only I understood and which, no matter how much I was begged, I would not decipher for anybody.

I remember one time when that Italian marquis who was so fond of fine arts, whom I think I spoke of to you on some occasion, visited me, the broken fountain sang, perhaps in his honor, with its most melodious and hidden voice, a long and captivating cantata with no beginning and no end.

"Who is singing, Madam?"

"My broken fountain, Marquis."

"And what is it saying?"

"Pardon me."

The Italian marquis, my son, who was very fond of the fine arts, above all music and poetry, insisted so much that I had to become harsh with him. In return for my discourtesy, my dear, I begged him to ask me for anything else within my reach, to try to please him, and the Italian marquis, Eliacim, undressed me and covered my body with whip lashes.

That broken fountain, my son, from which a long stream of water always trickles, was dry for three days. The scars of the whipping, I could still show them to you, Eliacim, if you asked me to.

Chapter 160: Viennese Waltzes

There was a time, Eliacim, when you and I liked Viennese waltzes, the forcibly happy Viennese waltzes, which are best listened to dressed as a tree and with the eyes half closed softly, with a feigned delicacy.

I remember, as if it were yesterday, the night you spent dancing Viennese waltzes with that insignificant girl whom I envied and hated with all the strength of my heart; with that insignificant girl, what was her name? who broke out crying, in the midst of a huge scandal, when you wanted to kiss her.

Viennese waltzes, Eliacim, are not favorable for love, we both know it. Viennese waltzes, my dear, are rather suited to becoming adept at the monotonous arts of marriage. Love, Eliacim, is arhythmical.

When I hear on the radio, by a not very strange coincidence, a Viennese waltz, Eliacim, "Waves of the Danube," for example, or "The Skaters," or "Voices of Spring," I take off my shoes and I jump over the furniture, my son, until I drop exhausted and almost breathless.

Then, Eliacim, I cry a little, in a fairly quiet way, and I kiss your photograph. Then, I usually fall asleep.

Yes, Eliacim, remember, there was a time, long ago now, when Viennese waltzes made you and me very happy, those desolating and happy Viennese waltzes, to which one must dance barefoot, or, in any case, in golden slippers.

In those days, my son, the blood which sailed through our veins, still smiled at us, and how traitorously! But that time, Eliacim, is now gone for both of us. It would be very difficult to go back and relive it, at least with the impetuosity of that time.

Chapter 161: The Bronze Bell Which Resounds over the Mountains

If I had enough power, Eliacim, I would order the bronze bell which resounds over the mountains to be silenced, because, when I am concentrating most and thinking of you, your eyes, for example, or the tone you put into your voice to ask me to prepare your bath for you, or the beauty mark which you had on your neck, or your inexpert hands, or, simply, that it's time to think about putting new strings on your tennis racket, it distracts me and obliges me, entirely against my will, to turn my back on you.

The bronze bell which resounds over the mountains, my son, I think could well be the bell of hatred, Eliacim, the bell which can never be silenced because it doesn't ring or toll in any place to which human beings can get without damning our souls forever, in the midst of the devil's rejoicing.

Among my friends or acquaintances in the neighborhood, my son, no one has ever heard the bronze bell which resounds over the mountains, and when I speak to them of it, Eliacim, they look at me with a strange gesture which bothers me. But the fact is that among my friends or acquaintances in the neighborhood, Eliacim, there are plenty who have a soul as deaf as a dead fish, a soul deaf and poisoned like a dead snake.

If I had the power, Eliacim, a really strong power and not a fictitious one, I would order the bronze bell which resounds over the mountains melted down, and with its feverish flesh, a statue to be erected in honor of stray animals. But I, my son, don't have any power; I, Eliacim, am nothing but a poor woman without any strength or power, without strength or power to throw to the ground, with a single gesture, even though in that gesture I had to compromise all my energy, the bronze bell which resounds over the mountains. If anything else were in my power, Eliacim, I would try to please you with it. In spite of your demands.

Chapter 162: The Child on Fire

I didn't want to put it out, my dear, because I didn't want the wrath of the gods unleashed on us, on you and on me.

The child on fire, Eliacim, surrounded by shouts, ran through the field igniting the ripe grain and over the mountain igniting the forests. The child on fire, Eliacim, who had pleasure painted on his face in indelible colors, ran along the shore igniting the ships and through the farms igniting the astonished cattle. The child on fire, Eliacim, whose name was Toby and who dressed in flames, was desperately pursued by women who wanted to put him out against their hearts, without any fear of the wrath of the gods.

He was an unforgettable spectacle, Eliacim, that child on fire. I woke up, startled, my dear, and I tried by every means to calm down, but his memory came back to me time and again as soon as I closed my eyes.

You, in the crowd, dressed in your uniform, and always handsome, although perhaps slightly older, were stupefied. The child on fire, announcing it with an exceedingly piercing whistle, was doing pirouettes in the air, up beyond the clouds, igniting the birds and the angels.

It was, as I told you, something which I will never be able to forget. But, how silly I am! Why am I explaining anything to you if you were there, in the crowd, dressed in your uniform and always handsome, although perhaps somewhat older, and stupefied?

Sometimes, my son, I have unpardonable lapses; yes, Eliacim, let's not deceive ourselves; I am no longer the woman I was.

Chapter 163: The Mother-of-Pearl Snail

Polished by the weeping of all of you, Eliacim, by your weeping and that of your companions, the glossy mother-of-pearl snail which I am caressing as I would pet the throat of a young girl, my dear, whistles at me, on my fingertips, with a softness for which I shall never be able to thank it enough.

Beside your picture, Eliacim, one of your pictures, the one in which you have a rose in your hand, underneath your picture, my dear, sleeps the mother-of-pearl snail when I, very late at night and very sadly, tire of caressing it.

The other night, Eliacim, the mother-of-pearl snail gave me a tremendous fright, a fright from which it took me several days to recover. I prefer not to tell you about it because, aside from the fact that, until I got to the end, you also would be frightened, the matter, fortunately, hadn't the slightest importance.

Chapter 164: The Oldest Tree in the City

It died of old age, Eliacim, so they say, the oldest tree in the city, the one in whose bark the captains who were departing for the Thirty Years' War carved the names of their sweethearts.

When I heard the news, my son, I thought I would become much sadder than, in fact, I later became.

I was fond of it, Eliacim, I should not tell you I wasn't, our old tree, the oldest tree in the city; but my heart, apparently, is hardening with the passage of time, becoming stiff with the swift course of pain.

I only gave the death of the oldest tree in the city, Eliacim, one day of tears, not counting mealtimes and the short time I did some shopping.

Its wood, which I bought from the city, will burn in my fireplace. What a pleasure, Eliacim, what a great pleasure!

Chapter 165: Street Musicians

With their accordion and violin, my son, the street musicians play in the doorways of taverns, in honor of the well-intentioned drinkers.

With their cornet and violin, my son, the street musicians play in the doorways of churches, in praise of the newlyweds who don't know how they will be able to live.

If it didn't cause gossiping, Eliacim, I would put all the street musicians I found playing polkas and marches in the doorways of taverns and churches in my house. Our house is large, my dear, as you know, and I think your mother and her street musicians would fit into it, her warm and aromatic street musicians, those who cover their heads with a cap with an oilcloth brim and those who have a lyre tattooed over their hearts. Street musicians, Eliacim, are usually heroes of the tiny tragedies which cast water over the life of men, perhaps so that the lowest spectators may be amused seeing how some men struggle against drowning.

But street musicians, Eliacim, who prefer to keep drowning little by little, like old whales, take no part in the fight they renounced in order to play music, from morning to night, while they wander slowly through the city, appearing at taverns and churches, in search of the kindly drinker and the poor groom who, almost by a miracle, can still give them enough for a meal.

On the cold days of winter, Eliacim, I think and think about the street musicians, the men who play sick violins, sick accordions, sick cornets and flutes, my son, and I feel a great remorse of conscience which I cannot avoid.

Yes, Eliacim; if it didn't cause gossip, I would fill our house with street musicians who, on April 17th, your birthday, would toast each other cheerfully and smilingly, and play, at the door of your empty room, the pieces which could please you most.

It would be a very happy day, Eliacim, an immensely happy day for everybody, but I don't have the courage, my son, I don't have, still! the necessary courage.

Chapter 166: The Unshipped Sailor Ashore

How sad is the unshipped sailor, Eliacim, the sailor who lost a leg on terra firma, run over by a train!

The unshipped sailor who lost his leg on terra firma, Eliacim, run over by the van, is named Eusebius W. Clownish; he has an aunt in South Dakota who is a nun; he is colored, although he swears he had a Majorcan grandfather; he tattoos skulls and sailing ships at reasonable rates; he trains parrots just for fun; he sings, with his eyes closed, sentimental songs of his country, and according to people who know him better than I, he can read Cervantes in the original.

The other day, Eliacim, I managed to talk for a long while

to Eusebius W. Clownish, the unshipped sailor who came to the house to offer himself to me, in case I wanted to be tattooed with an anchor, a flower, which is proper for women, a palm tree, some initials. Although there was a moment, my dear, when I thought I would tattoo my belly with the letters E. A. C., intertwined, I preferred not to because it didn't seem to me, on second thought, that it was of any use.

"Good sailor, how did you lose your leg?"

"Ah, ma'am, I wish I knew! Some say that it was the train, ma'am, which always goes along its tracks; some say, ma'am, that it was a van, which sometimes, especially in narrow streets, mounts the sidewalk. . ."

The unshipped sailor, my dear, fills me with fright. I couldn't imagine that there was anyone in the world as sad as Eusebius W. Clownish, the unshipped sailor who lost his leg on terra firma, and I made him a cup of hot tea.

"A little cake?"

"Yes, ma'am, thank you."

I gave the unshipped sailor a cake and a half, Eliacim.

"More tea?"

"Yes, ma'am, thank you."

I served the unshipped sailor some twenty cups of tea, Eliacim.

"A cigarette?"

"Yes, ma'am, thank you."

The unshipped sailor smoked up all the cigarettes I had in the house, Eliacim.

"Gin?"

"No, ma'am, thank you, I don't drink."

The unshipped sailor who lost a leg on terra firma, Eliacim, seemed to me, for a few moments, perhaps, somewhat less sad.

139

Chapter 167: Thirst

If I had an enormous, permanent thirst, my son, I would be drinking all day, and my recollections, perhaps, would be kinder and more receptive. But, the way things are! I have almost no thirst, and it is immensely difficult work for me to drink. (With this lack of thirst of mine, Eliacim, my recollections are, generally, desolate and have a black perspective.)

Thirst, Eliacim, is the cable which Providence stretches out to the affectionate, the poor, the sick, to those who, like me, although it may have been denied to me, live, with their backs resting as if by a miracle, between inertia and chance.

Thirst, my son, is a word which I ought not dare to pronounce before you, for you are thirsty in the midst of so much water, but which, although I know the harm I am doing to you, I cannot keep quiet either.

Chapter 168: The Fanciful Low Neckline of Matilda Help

Matilda Help, my dear, has a fanciful and low neckline down which history glides: Alexander, Julius Caesar, Napoleon, Victor Hugo. Matilda Help, my son, you weren't able to know her, which is a real shame, is the illegitimate daughter of a Polish countess who is always very ready to aid the poor, and an R.A.F. pilot, who was shot down over enemy territory and who was never heard from again.

Matilda Help, my dear, could not know her father, whom her mother, no doubt, would have married, and she has to be content with seeing how history (Hannibal, Christopher Columbus, Chateaubriand, Bismarck) glides down her deep and fanciful low neckline.

Matilda Help, my dear, is already two years old and she speaks with a striking clarity. It fills me with joy when her mother, a Polish countess always ready to aid the destitute, brings her to the house to pay a call.

Chapter 169: Dismissal from School

Every day in the morning, Eliacim, I read the news section of the paper very carefully, to see how many children have died from being run over at dismissal from school. Though it may seem surprising to you, Eliacim, almost never do children die from being run over at school dismissal, and this is a mystery I will never manage to clear up.

School dismissal, my dear, with so many defenseless savages at liberty jumping between the cars and vans, is a depressing spectacle for a civilized country.

I don't know if it would be better, Eliacim, more convenient for everybody, if drivers received very strict and definite orders to run over two or three children every other day to see if we could put an end to so much unbounded senseless joy. The teachers have already shown to the limit their lack of ability in this.

I don't know if the publishers of newspapers, harboring in their hearts improper and poorly understood feelings of philanthropy, have ordered their editors to throw into the wastebasket all news referring to these always plausible infantile accidents, because I cannot fathom, my dear, how half a dozen boys and the same number of girls do not die every day, run over at dismissal from school by cars and vans.

Perhaps it is better for this to happen this way, but perhaps also the hour has already arrived for the application of the serious remedies which are usually necessary to meet serious evils.

Chapter 170: The Embers of the Hearth

When the light is out, Eliacim, a little before going to sleep, I usually stay awhile watching the embers in the hearth, the red, blue, orange, pink, green, pale violet embers, left by the firewood burned during the day.

Some lucky nights, Eliacim, among the last sparks of the embers in the fireplace, you appear, with your eyes closed, and you speak a few words to me in a strange language which I cannot understand, a strange language which perhaps could be Greek.

The nights when this happens, not often unfortunately, I don't get into bed until the embers turn black and gray, my dear, like the smoke and fog on the docks, and cold like that hand which we always fear finding.

If one could eat the fireplace embers, Eliacim, if one could eat them just like *foie gras* or butter, spreading them on toast, I would never go to bed without trying to eat you, my dear, although later you might speak in your strange language inside of me, and the women who came to call would think me a monster capable of devouring Greek sailors, or Greek sponge fishermen, or Greek poets, or self-absorbed Greek soldiers in crisp white skirts.

But the fireplace embers, Eliacim, are something which we must be satisfied merely to stare at, sometimes almost deceitfully, so that they may keep giving back to us, little by little, that burning son whom we mothers all lost, perhaps so that we should feel ashamed to keep listening to the excruciating beat of our hearts.

The embers in the hearth, Eliacim, with their delicate breathing which dies away with such a handy slowness, tie me at night, my dear, to the hours when I ought to be dreaming of you and of nothing but you, and resist releasing me as if I, poor me! were still desirable prey.

Chapter 171: Typewriters

If I had a few extra pounds, Eliacim, I would buy myself a typewriter so I could spend the day striking the keys, even if only in a disordered and arbitrary way.

I think, Eliacim, that typewriters are the most mysterious objects in existence, objects which bring man and woman closer to the ugly angels who would not be content with their fate.

If I had a typewriter, my son, I would clean it carefully every morning, so that no one could reproach me for carelessness, and, if I thought it were discreet and capable of keeping a secret, I would write my letters to you on it, Eliacim, so that it would be easier for you to read them and also so that you could show them, from a distance, to your friends.

Chapter 172: Ancient Books

Ancient books, my son, as those who know assure us, are veritable wells of wisdom which jealously guard their water which is not given to all those who want to drink it, but only to very select thirsty people, the thirsty people who from the cradle onward have had their flesh molded by the flexible and spongy wood with which the wise are made.

Ancient books, Eliacim, with their letters now pale from having been read and reread so many times, hide beneath their dirty exteriors, the mouth of the deep cave where the keys to wisdom are kept, those heavy keys which so few dare to carry upon their shoulders.

When you were going along the road of wisdom, Eliacim, and even though you were ignorant of everything, you looked like you could come to know everything, I dreamt of being able to give you an ancient book which would give you the key to all things, an ancient book which would explain to you, on a solid footing, the clearest mysteries of the universe.

But now that ancient books are of no use to you, Eliacim, because at the bottom of the sea things are foretold which the ancient books fail to clarify, I reject ancient books.

And I'm on the verge of swearing that they contain only painful lies.

Chapter 173: Hands

Oh, my son! if we only knew what hands are good for, with their thousand tiny bones, their fingers, their nails, their palms, their backs! Oh, my son! if we could only use our hands to hold the thing which we wanted never to let go of! Oh, my son! if hands could be used, at least, to say goodbye! Oh, my son! if hands were not so useless, so cruel, and forgetful! Oh, my son! if our hands were made of the same smooth glass as our hearts!

Hands, Eliacim, these hands of mine which I'm looking at now, full of strangeness and astonishment, as if they were the hands of a woman decapitated by the French Revolution; these hands which I wash several times during the day; these hands which, by dint of care, are still well preserved; these blind hands which one day served to comb your hair, today seem dead and useless. If hands could be bought and sold, my dear, I should not hesitate an instant to trade these hands of mine for other, happier hands, for other hands which would know that they are useful for something, necessary for some rubescent or pallid enterprise.

But our hands, Eliacim, adhere to misfortune, with the strength with which the traitorous wind adheres to the sails of the ship, and we can not tear them away, as if with the blow of an axe, so that they will poison the hungriest dogs with our poison.

Oh yes we can, Eliacim, but we haven't the courage to do it; God knows!

Our hands, my son, are only good for us to spend the day looking at them, front and back, to feel that we are, with each hour that passes, a little more, prisoners of their worst and most premeditated intentions.

Oh, my son, what a disgrace it is to know what our hands are for, with their hundred tiny bones, their fingers, their nails!

Chapter 174: The Fish without Scales

It was a fish without scales, a fish as smooth, soft and nameless as a girl. When I brought him home, thinking that you would have liked very much to caress him slowly, my dear, I noticed in myself a giddiness, like an almost imperceptible vertigo, which made me very happy; why should I lie to you?

The fish without scales, Eliacim, my fish without scales, was a beautiful orange color which later softened little by little, perhaps from sadness, perhaps by contagion with the sadness to which I am condemned, this sadness which only very occasionally my orange-colored fish without scales was able to soothe.

On top of the mantelpiece, Eliacim, the fish without scales resembled a sick girl, a dying girl, a girl who had a crow's nest lying on her fragile ribs, next to the most fickle partitions of her heart.

I tried with my breath to revive the fish without scales, Eliacim, but the fish without scales, with his mouth wide open and his expressionless eyes, slipped out of my hand and killed himself on the floor, my son, he probably killed himself on the floor.

(I think, Eliacim, that the fish without scales, had he been more docile, would not have found the painless, gloryless death of the suicides from high towers, those sentimental birds whose air fails them in mid-flight.)

Exceedingly sad over the death of my fish without scales, my dear, I kept him by my side as long as I could, until he began to smell very badly and his beautiful and bright orange color softened and got darker like the wrath of the gentlest birds. Then, Eliacim, I sat down on the floor, I know very well it was so that my legs wouldn't shake, and I threw him into the fire in the fireplace, a fire which took a long time to devour him, much more time than I would have thought.

The fish without scales, my son, crackled like an insect numb with cold and became a colorless flame, a little, almost invisible flame. And that considering that my fish without scales was a smooth fish, Eliacim, a soft and nameless fish like a girl who feels herself embraced by a very strong man.

Chapter 175: The Little Marble Figurine

You were happy with the marble figurine in your pocket, Eliacim, without knowing, perhaps, that the marble figurine which had the patina of age, contained the soul of a Chinese prostitute of the Sung dynasty who had been very unhappy after having known happiness.

And you didn't know, Eliacim, and it surely was not I who unveiled the mystery for you, that that marble figurine which later ended up getting lost, contained in the remotest and darkest corner of its awareness, the memory of various horrible crimes committed by the weak of every age, by the most pallid and smiling murderers of every age.

You were radiant with the marble figurine in your pocket, Eliacim, and you asked me to pet it, something I refused to do despite your threats. It was a difficult moment for me, my dear, very hard, a moment which tired me in an unusual way, because I had to make a great effort to say no to you, Eliacim, to tell you that all your attempts to make me pet the marble figurine were perfectly useless.

I felt a great relief, my son, the day when I couldn't find the marble figurine no matter how hard I looked. Luckily, although only in this case, you were not with me; I don't even want to think about what would have happened, with you in the next room.

Because you, Eliacim, had placed your greatest affection in that marble figurine which ended up getting lost. You even, my son, exercised a firmer and purer love with her than that which you had for your mother, who neither was marble nor harbored the soul of a remote Chinese prostitute of the Sung dynasty (960–1279), a remote Chinese prostitute who knew the flowering of the arts.

Chapter 176: I Am Not Unaware of Your Most Hidden Thoughts

I am not unaware of your most hidden thoughts, Eliacim, although, frequently, when you are premeditatedly cold with me, I would be better off not having the faculty of knowing them as if you carried them written in ink on your forehead.

Your most hidden, most secret thoughts, my dear, could be grouped in three separate classes:

(a) Thoughts in which you imagine making obvious your love toward everything which surrounds me, so as to try to enclose me in a cold island of indifference.

(b) Thoughts in which you think to make me understand that I am an obstacle in your life and that you are attempting by all the means at your command to get rid of all the obstacles in your path.

(c) Thoughts in which you openly wish for my death.

(These last thoughts, Eliacim, sometimes make you sad;

then, you usually cloak them in a small gift, some flowers, some bon bons, a box of powder.)

I am not unaware of your most hidden and veiled thoughts, Eliacim. Imagine how painful it is to write these lines.

Chapter 177: In a Bottle Floating on the Sea

When I look at the green sea, Eliacim, I always think I see bottles floating, bottles with a desperate message hidden in their bellies.

In a bottle floating in the sea, Eliacim, may be your last five or six words which you couldn't say to me in my ear, with no one in the room, with nobody bothering us by their presence.

The bottles which are launched by the shipwrecked, with a smile inside, in the turbulent waters of the sea, Eliacim, become, when the years pass over them, the females of the shark, fierce females of the swift and bloody male shark.

There have been bottles, my son, bottles which still float without reaching any beach, over which hang all the curses for not allowing themselves to become, bit by bit, the females of the shark, according to the old maritime laws.

I don't know, Eliacim, if there is a collection of marine bottles in the world, bottles which served to keep alive, for a few moments, the little flame of hope in the most disillusioned hearts. But if there were, my son, and I came to know of it, I would travel at once to the remotest parts to see it and be able to embrace its owner who, perhaps, would be an old man who enjoyed telling fantastic and unlikely stories about big-game hunting.

Chapter 178: The Iceberg

My dear son:
Sailing without compass, the iceberg flies, with you on top, at an incredible speed.

The iceberg flies, with you on top, at an incredible speed, sailing without compass.

With you on top, the iceberg flies, sailing without compass, at an incredible speed.

At an incredible speed, with you on top, the iceberg flies, sailing without compass.

Sailing without compass, the iceberg flies, at an incredible speed, with you on top.

The iceberg flies, with you on top, sailing without compass, at an incredible speed.

With you on top, the iceberg flies, at an incredible speed, sailing without compass.

At an incredible speed, the iceberg flies, with you on top, sailing without compass.

Sailing without compass, with you on top, the iceberg flies, at an incredible speed.

The iceberg flies, at an incredible speed, with you on top, sailing without compass.

With you on top, at an incredible speed, sailing without compass, the iceberg flies.

At an incredible speed, with you on top, sailing without compass, the iceberg flies.

Sailing without compass, at an incredible speed, the iceberg flies, with you on top.

The iceberg flies, at an incredible speed, sailing without compass, with you on top.

Sailing without compass, with you on top, at an incredible speed, the iceberg flies.

With you on top, at an incredible speed, the iceberg flies, sailing without compass.

At an incredible speed, the iceberg flies, sailing without compass, with you on top.

The iceberg flies, sailing without compass, with you on top, at an incredible speed.

With you on top, sailing without compass, the iceberg flies, at an incredible speed.

At an incredible speed, sailing without compass, the iceberg flies, with you on top.

Sailing without compass, at an incredible speed, with you on top, the iceberg flies.

The iceberg flies, sailing without compass, at an incredible speed, with you on top.

With you on top, sailing without compass, at an incredible speed, the iceberg flies.

At an incredible speed, sailing without compass, with you on top, the iceberg flies.

I always remember, Eliacim, that you worried a lot about icebergs, routes, photographs, customs, the flora and fauna of the white, pale rose, and sky-blue icebergs which flee like eloping brides through the Arctic seas.

Chapter 179: The Miser

I.

With his nard stick in his hand, Eliacim, and his thick glass spectacles, the miser sits very still so as not to spend himself, while his children dream about the sandwiches at his funeral, the effusive and sincere congratulations of the funeral.

The miser, Eliacim, has transparent skin, like very young infants, and his head is inhabited by industrious worms, expert in the most various occupations, those of blacksmith, carpenter, gravedigger, woodcutter, fisherman, chimney-sweep.

With his little Mercury wings on his heels, Eliacim, and his cap of frayed green velvet embroidered with gold oak leaves, the miser moves very cautiously, my dear, so as not to spend himself while the children in the street squander evil feelings, and run, and jump, and shout ceaselessly, under his window.

The miser, Eliacim, has wet eyes like the eyes of sick cats, and his chest is inhabited by well-known sounds, the symbol of all the sensations which he kept saving, with utmost care, for the long and uncertain years of his old age.

With his little star painted on his forehead, Eliacim, and his luxurious although now a little old slippers, the miser, my son, died without anyone noticing.

2.

I wish you had been a miser, Eliacim, an old miser laden with years and with riches, like the miser who died the other day, without anyone noticing, opening the joy valve of those who lived with him.

Chapter 180: The Enchanted Garden

If you had gotten lost in an abandoned garden, Eliacim, in a murky garden of willows and junipers, I would never tire of looking for you, my dear, of looking for you with lights, and with the little hazelwood wand which illuminates the waters and hidden treasures, and with a timid inexhaustible hope, until I had come upon you, perhaps changed into a blade of grass.

How happy are the mothers who lose their sons in abandoned gardens, Eliacim, in the gardens inhabited by shadows and by words nobody listens to! They have the consolation, my son, of continuing to look, look always, look ceaselessly with the hope of being able to touch, some day, unexpectedly, their own heart!

Not very far from the house in which I was born, Eliacim, there was an abandoned garden, a murky garden of willows and junipers, through which mothers who had lost their sons walked and talked alone and senselessly, from morning to night, without one person approaching them to ask if they needed anything.

(As I was a very little girl, Eliacim, I laughed venomously, and fell asleep thinking warmly about them.)

God's punishment, Eliacim, was worse than I expected, my dear, because I don't even have, after so many vain illusions, an abandoned garden in which to search for you ceaselessly from morning to night, with lights, with the little hazelwood wand that illuminates the waters and hidden treasures, with a timid inexhaustible hope.

Chapter 181: Honey

Your decisiveness seemed as if it were going to have an outlet in other directions, my son, in harder, more elegant, more violent directions; but, despite your evident decisiveness, you limited yourself to saying: "From tomorrow on I must have honey for lunch; it's a substance which fortifies the body and prolongs life." Fine, my son, you will have honey for lunch. And that was that.

You tired very quickly, Eliacim, of honey; that's the truth. Honey is cloying to the palate and heavy in the stomach. Honey is somewhat too natural, too elemental for a city man.

I didn't want to say: "Do you see? Didn't I tell you (I could have told you) that you would end up not being able to stand honey?" I didn't want to tell you, my son, for two reasons: to avoid your being able to answer me angrily, an ugly habit which I tried to get you out of at every opportunity, and because I, my dearest son, always, always kept quiet about anything that I suspected could hurt you.

Honey, Eliacim, is something much stronger, compact, and consistent than the souls of city boys, although these city boys, my dear, may have athletic pretensions, on occasion, as you used to then.

Honey, Eliacim, is the food of dark and coarse forest bears, of the blackish, coarse forest woodcutters, of the cruel, coarse hunters of forest bears. And never, my son, of the young men who sometimes read Lord Byron attentively.

Many were the things which you had still to learn, Eliacim. I think your desertion was as hasty as it was premature.

Chapter 182: A Completely Uninteresting Burial

I can assure you, Eliacim, that it was a completely uninteresting burial, a boring and gray burial like the afternoons of winter, a burial with too much cold and too little emotion.

Of course, the body didn't deserve it, that's true, but even so, I think that they could have gotten more out of it, had the family bothered a bit, something which they did not do.

If you had still been at home, Eliacim, you would have attended the burial in my place. The bad part of it is that, upon your return, with your flesh decomposed and your soul depressed, you would surely have felt within your rights in scolding me for having begged you to go to such a boring and inane burial.

"Bad luck, my son, bad luck! But just think that neither you nor I am to blame for the burial of poor Mr. Quaking turning out, in fact, to be a completely uninteresting burial."

"You could have figured as much."

"In spite of everything, Eliacim, in spite of everything."

I can assure you, Eliacim, as I was saying, that it was a completely uninteresting burial, a boring and circumspect burial like the speech of a Minister, a tasteless burial without distinguished guests. Poor Mr. Quaking is ready to be received in the other world just as he was ushered out of this one, Eliacim, I can tell you.

Chapter 183: Color Photographs

When I look at your color photographs, Eliacim, a field full of white and yellow daisies, a sorrel mare with her colt by her side, a girl dressed in cretonne, I always smile as if I were, poor me! a very experienced woman.

Your color photographs, Eliacim, your photographs in artificial and conventional colors, my son, seem like dried flowers when looked at against the light, flowers which never saw the fresh air like the flowers we see every day, like garden flowers, flowers which were born in the greenhouses which are looked after, with a double door which prevents air currents, by the most skillful dryers of flowers, those men of iron feelings who do not know the color of condescension, the tenuous color of mercy.

Your color photographs, my son, your ingenuous color photographs, with which you so entertained the silly girls of the neighborhood, Eliacim, I keep under lock and key so as not to have to feel obligated to smile when I see them.

Chapter 184: That Vase Which Broke into a Thousand Pieces

I very much admired that vase which, on your first anniversary, my son, broke into a thousand pieces without anyone's touching it. It wasn't authentic (I know) but it had a graceful line, and a bird of paradise, with seven feathers with the colors of the rainbow in its tail, which gave it a marvelous appearance, a shining and proud presence.

Although at first I thought I would keep the pieces and stick them together, one by one, with the greatest of care, later, when I saw that putting them together was impossible, I decided to throw the pieces, one by one, into the garbage. Finally, Eliacim, I picked them up, one by one, I wrapped them up, one by one, each one in its tissue paper, and I hid them in the drawer of my cabinet, without anyone seeing me, so as not to have to keep explaining to people what doesn't concern them.

On your anniversaries always, Eliacim, and on the other

days, when I feel even more alone than usually, I shut myself up in my room, and I open the cabinet humming some little song to pretend, and I contemplate and I caress, one by one, the thousand pieces of that beautiful vase which broke, without anyone's touching it, the day of your first anniversary.

(I have observed, Eliacim, that the pieces of the broken vase are warm, very warm, on your anniversaries, and later, little by little, they keep getting colder, until the anniversary of the following year, when they again have a fever. Perhaps, my dear, this is a supernatural effect; in any case, I don't know how to interpret it.)

The great admiration I had for that vase which on your first anniversary, my son, broke into a thousand pieces without anyone's touching it, has gradually been leaving me. Now, what I admire greatly are its pieces.

Chapter 185: Swedish Matches

Swedish matches are famous the world over, Eliacim, as the matches which never fail. If I had had occasion to give you a boatload of Swedish matches, Eliacim, be assured that I would not have wasted it.

(Now I think: what could you have done, Eliacim, with a boatload of Swedish matches? Horrors! You could have been the general representative for Swedish matches in London, for one entire day. Would London consume a boatload of Swedish matches a day? I don't know.)

Swedish matches, my son, enjoy a well-earned reputation in all the markets of the world, in all the markets of the five continents. In spite of the rumors which circulated persistently a few years ago—you were very young—Swedish matches enjoy a well-earned reputation in all the markets of the world. And what is more important: they know how to maintain it.

Chapter 186: The Bread We Eat

Man plows and fertilizes, sows and weeds the earth, harvests the ripe grain, mills the grain, kneads the flour, cooks the bread and sells it to us. What great stupidity!

Bread, my son, is the most topical and trite symbol of nutrition: man's soul is not omnivorous, Eliacim. We want bread! shout the hungry. I earn my daily bread honestly, say the poor public officials. I will give you bread, announces the besieging army to the besieged position, if you surrender within such and such a time; if not, I will give you iron, immense clouds of iron. (Iron, in a certain sense, is the most topical and trite symbol of death and destruction.)

The bread we eat, my son, is a dirty product of advertising, a noxious food for the body and for the memory, the understanding, and the will.

Great men, Eliacim, never ate bread, or, if they did eat it, it was always with great caution and deliberation, because, bread, my son, brutalizes the feelings, and sometimes poisons organisms and plunges people into madness.

The cases of allergy to bread, which usually manifest themselves in an eczema which runs along the arms and legs, are not infrequent.

Eliacim, we shouldn't eat the bread we eat. The legislator of the future will prohibit the consumption of bread.

Chapter 187: Sybaritism

You used to show a certain inclination toward sybaritism, Eliacim, a certain fondness which could never in any case seem bad to me. The education of children, Eliacim, ought to tend, in my opinion, to inculcate in them the norms of what, if they do not find out in time, they later learn in a disorderly way and to no one's advantage, and even to serious disadvantage for themselves.

To live according to the demanding dictates of nonconformity, Eliacim, is highly educational, exceptionally formative. In men who reach the highest positions, my son, one can usually observe these salutary principles, these rigid and implacable norms of maladaptation and of rigorous and almost cruel domination.

It would be curious to know the statistics on patients and sybarites in relation to the positions they manage to occupy in society. (Also, the possibility of the inverse process can be admitted, certainly, but I believe, Eliacim, that power induces sybaritism less than sybaritism power. It would be a question, perhaps, deserving of treatment with greater attention and detail.)

The sybarite, Eliacim, and you were on the way to becoming one, carries a little mirror in his heart to try to reflect, in his own pride, the world of others. The one who conforms to everything, my son, despite what might appear to people who are not attentive to this problem, bears a spiny thistle, or a cruel sea urchin, in his heart.

It would have made me very proud, Eliacim, to manage to make a sybarite of you, a man who, walking along the street with his head high and without looking at anybody, would make people exclaim: "Look, there goes a sybarite, you can tell by his bearing, by the way he walks, in a certain something which true sybarites have."

But, my son, always the same thing, I have to content myself with knowing that you are a hero. What can we do!

Chapter 188: A Bloodstain on the Pillow

My son, on your mother's pillow there appears every morning a little bloodstain. Although at first it worried me, because I didn't know its origin, now that I know it, I feel even so as if it is keeping me company. The blood on your mother's pillow, my dear, comes from her lung; I cough while I sleep, and spit blood, a little tiny stain, oval-shaped, which is dry and opaque when I wake up.

The doctor's diagnosis gave me very little hope, Eliacim, but I have become accustomed to the idea that I am not to live for many useless years to no purpose.

The bloodstain on my pillow, my dear, usually resembles you. I consulted a few people who claim to have known you well, Eliacim, and I was able to confirm sadly that all of them have forgotten how you were, your profile, the cut of your face, the picture of the unruly lock of hair which used to fall over your forehead.

Your portraits in blood, Eliacim, I cut them out carefully, and so that they do not ravel, I usually make a little hem all around them; this is how I spend almost my whole day now.

In my will, my son, I have added a clause providing that they wrap me in a shroud made by sewing together all the portraits of you which I spit out each morning.

It is somewhat toilsome, I know, but I am leaving

twenty-five pounds to whoever will lend himself to the task. Someone will appear.

And no one can say that I am abandoning any of the things I most love in this world, Eliacim, those silhouettes of you which I make for you, in my veins, night after night.

Chapter 189: The Sentimental Tailor

Near our house, Eliacim, a very sentimental Syrian tailor has installed himself, who cries when it's cold and gives the girls bluebells when spring arrives. His prices, my son, are not at all cheap, but rather are somewhat dearer than those of the other tailors, but people have taken a liking to him, because he is very good and very sentimental, and his clientele is growing constantly.

The Syrian tailor, my son, is named Joshua, and has a black, very shiny mane, which falls as if disdainfully to his shoulders.

Joshua, my son, has a wooden leg, but he doesn't want to say where he lost it, nor how, nor when; as for me, I think, Eliacim, that Joshua came into the world missing a leg, because when anyone asks him: "Joshua, where and how and when did you become lame?" he bursts out crying disconsolately, as he does when it's cold.

The other day, Eliacim, I spoke to Joshua about the Aegean Sea and again he cried. To reward him somewhat I had him cut me an almost shapeless suit, but this morning, when I went to try it on, he saw that he had measured wrong and again he burst out crying. Joshua, my son, is such a sentimental Syrian tailor, that he spends more than half his life crying.

"Is it all the same to you if the suit is a little tight?"

Your mother, my dear, is already past the age of coquetry, and has been for several years.

"All right, if it's not too tight!"

Joshua cried again.

"Oh, it is, ma'am, it is rather! Oh, what tremendous misfortune besets me!"

I tried to console him, Eliacim.

"Don't worry, Joshua; it's all the same to me if the suit is tight on me; what I wanted to do was help you, you seem to me a very nice tailor."

Joshua threw himself on the floor choking with tears.

"Ah, charity, always charity, and not the reward of an artist!"

I, Eliacim, paid him for the suit and left it in the shop. Truly, even though I had weighed twenty pounds less and measured twenty inches less, I wouldn't have fit into it.

Chapter 190: Let's See, Let's See?

When you said to me, Let's see, let's see? although I submissively showed you what you wanted to see, I felt myself invaded by rage. You were very lucky, my dear, that I never showed it to you violently, something which later, without doubt, I would have regretted, because around that time, I was tremendously strong, with a strength capable of knocking down a bull with two or three blows.

The curiosity you showed for everything, my son, the sick curiosity which you showed for everything except the things relating to me, Eliacim, was something which finally threatened to destroy you. I stopped making you see it that way, because I knew well enough that advice, no matter how prudent and sage it was, didn't go well with your indomitable character. (Your character, my son, was always so placid and kind that not even now, when I deny it to you even knowing that I am lying, my dearest, do you interrupt me with a let's see, let's see?)

I can understand, Eliacim, that young people have a desire to learn, an eagerness to keep clarifying and deciphering everything which surrounds them, everything that they keep discovering daily, and to this end you all ask, constantly, Let's see, let's see? but also I would like to see myself repaid and to know that young people, at least young people like you, Eliacim, are getting to see that the impertinent Let's see, let's see? is something which can make a saint lose patience.

When you used to say to me, my son, Let's see, let's see? putting on a beatific gesture of regret, I suddenly wanted to strangle you, or at least throw you out of the house so that you would face the harsh reality of life. You were always saved from an exemplary punishment by the great affection which your mother always had for you, at times even against our own, common interest, which is the thing which for both of us ought to be above everything else in this world.

Because, look at it this way, my dear, youth gets out of line if it is not brought up short, if it is not kept firmly in hand.

And the duty of a mother, Eliacim, even though it is as in this case a painful and difficult one to fulfill, ought not to take second place to any other consideration. Because of forgetting this, human affairs are drifting, my dear, toward being smashed against the rocks of war and against other punishments of God.

Chapter 191: I Feel Desperate, Although Not Enthusiastically Desperate

I think it must be horrible to feel desperate with enthusiasm, Eliacim, to feel desperate with all the crevices of hope blocked up with the stuff of hate, with the viscous and impermeable paste of hate.

But I, my son, luckily, although I feel desperate, don't feel desperate with enthusiasm, don't feel desperate with grandeur, irremediably, like the high waves of the sea, the wind which flees across the mountains, or the solitary marten which scratches his leprosy against the roughest bark in the forest.

The desperation of the materfamilias, Eliacim, although, as happens with me, these mothers may have been left without families, never attains sublime overtones, the exceedingly noble accents of the desperation of forgotten virgins, my dear, hearts which despair enthusiastically, Eliacim, like drunken ballet dancers whom the police accuse of spying for the Germans.

Yes, Eliacim, I feel desperate, blindly, humbly desperate, but it gives me a great interior peace to know that I am not desperate with enthusiasm, like old butterflies which didn't find a corner suitable for the weaving of their cocoon of soft silk, and which pale in the sun, like colored cloth, while the moon continues on its gentle way.

Chapter 192: Three Fat Turkish Ladies

Holding hands, Eliacim, the three fat Turkish ladies went shopping. The number one fat Turkish lady bought herself a rubber girdle. The number two fat Turkish lady bought herself some patent leather shoes and a rubber girdle. The number three fat Turkish lady, who was no doubt the richest, bought herself a stylish purse, some patent leather shoes with a silver buckle, and a rubber girdle. The three fat Turkish ladies walked in silence, holding hands, afraid perhaps of being run down by an automobile or by a motorcycle while they went shopping, Eliacim.

The other night, my son, I dreamt of three fat ladies who I thought were Turkish until someone, more knowledgeable than I in the almost secret science which studies races, assured me that they were Yebalic and that one was called Amina, which means faithful, the next Zohora, which means pure, and the last Aixa, which is the same as vital.

As is logical, Eliacim, Amina was content with the rubber girdle, Zohora decided to go as far as the shoes, and Aixa was the fattest and the best-off of the three. Doesn't it seem, Eliacim, like a fable?

If sometime I dream again about the three fat Turkish ladies, Eliacim, who go shopping, holding hands, I promise to keep you informed of what happens to them. You ought to trust me, my dear, since you know I have always kept my word.

Chapter 193: The Old Garnet-Colored Silk Curtain

The old garnet-colored silk curtain on which I dry my tears, Eliacim, has begun to ravel in some places. The truth, Eliacim, is that although it was already old when you came into the world, I always remember it in my mother's house, I can't get used to the idea that it might die before me; I always wanted to believe that it was to last forever and, of course, much longer than me. How boring, Eliacim, to think that everything, without exception, dies and disappears.

Behind our old garnet-colored silk curtain, Eliacim, you hid when you were little, and you played ghosts while I pretended not to find you and to get very frightened at the strange noises which were heard all through the house. What times they were, Eliacim, excuse me, how recent they still seem to me!

Our old garnet-colored silk curtain, Eliacim—you can see that its hour has come—has begun to ravel in some places. I tell it: Don't worry, as old as you are I will not make you leave my side. And I ask it: Is it true that you always prefer to stay in the house, although in the house there may not be the happiness today that there was at another time? But the old garnet-colored silk curtain, Eliacim, our old curtain, perhaps mute from fear, doesn't answer me. Perhaps it doesn't know English; I, at least, never heard it speak it.

Chapter 194: The Feelings of Wood

Do you know, Eliacim, the feelings of wood, the love, the responsibility, the fear, the hatred, the loyalty, the purity of wood?

(That conversation which we had about this entertaining topic, Eliacim, do you remember? that we interrupted because some friends came for you to go to the horse races, we could continue it, if you like, some day when you have a couple of idle hours.)

I don't think that anyone has ever stopped to think, with his mind prepared for any and all surprises, about this business of the feelings of wood, abstract and diffuse like the feelings of men, but in no case more abstract and diffuse than the feelings of men.

And it is a shame what I have just told you, Eliacim, because to know the feelings of wood, my son, could turn out very profitably for everyone. It is not the same thing, Eliacim, notice this, to eat at a table of loyal wood, as to eat at a table of cowardly wood; to sleep in a bed of pure wood, as to sleep in a bed of irresponsible wood; to be buried in a coffin of amorous wood, as to be buried in a coffin of vengeful wood.

What a shame, Eliacim, not to be able to take private instruction in the means of knowing the feelings of wood!

Chapter 195: The Astronomy Student

Pale and trembling, Eliacim, the astonomy student walked, holding hands with his sweetheart, beneath the high stars, as he should.

"Will you love me forever, Rose?"

"I will love you forever, Patrick."

"Even though they fail me for not knowing how to find the azimuthal coordinates of Bellatrix?"

"Even though they fail you for not knowing how to find the azimuthal coordinates of Bellatrix."

"How good you are, Rose!"

Rose sighed vigorously.

("Don't shout so!")

Rose sighed delicately.

"No, Patrick; it's not that I'm good, it's that I love you!"

With his features out of joint, and his face colorless, Eliacim, the astonomy student walked and walked, holding his sweetheart around the waist, beneath the high moon, as you can imagine.

"Will you always be faithful, Rose?"

"I will always be faithful, Patrick."

"Even though they fail me because I can't calculate the degrees, minutes, and seconds of the right ascension of Algenib?"

"Even though they flunk you because you can't calculate the degrees, minutes, and seconds of the right ascension of Algenib."

The astronomy student kissed his sweetheart on the eyelids.

"How good you are, Rose!"

Rose sighed violently.

("Shhhhhh!")

Rose sighed timidly.

"No, Patrick; it's not that I'm good, it's that I love you so much!"

Bent over, gaunt, and coughing, Eliacim, the astronomy student walked and walked, up and down, with his sweetheart seated on one shoulder, beneath the closest constellations, as you can well believe without much effort.

Chapter 196: Everything Very Simple

Everything is very simple, Eliacim, astonishingly simple. A woman is born, grows up, marries, goes shopping, has a son, deceives her husband, apparently takes care of her home, loses her son, does works of charity, gets bored, and dies. And thus, once, and again, and yet again, my dear.

Everything is so simple, Eliacim, everything turns out so

simply in the end that at times I think that only great murderers deserve to benefit from the immense peace which usually settles in their look, in that happy look which didn't believe in the simplicity of things, my son, in the dull simplicity of adultery, in the daily simplicity of usury, in the diaphanous simplicity of bestiality.

If our first parents, Adam and Eve, Eliacim, had not been expelled from Paradise, perhaps, at this late date, human beings wouldn't be obliged to feel ourselves so wickedly simple.

Yes, Eliacim, yes; everything is very simple, everything is overwhelmingly simple. A man is born, grows up, learns a trade, marries, tries to earn more money every day, has a son, is deceived by his wife (which does not displease him), goes to his club in the afternoons, loses his son, tells marvelous lies about the war, or about his hunting expeditions in Tanganyika, gets bored, and dies. And thus once, twice, thrice, four times.

(There are men, nevertheless, Eliacim, who drown when their trade is still newly learned.)

Chapter 197: The People Who Pass in the Street

From behind the window shades, Eliacim, I see how the people who pass in the street hustle back and forth, and die.

The people who pass in the street, my son, are not varied and amusing, as one would expect, but boring, resigned, monotonous. The people who pass in the street, Eliacim, with their debts, their stomach ulcers, their family problems, their insane, miraculous plans, etc., walk with their spirits cowed, in no particular direction, with the secret hope that death will catch them by surprise, like the ax murderer who waits in ambush at the doors of schools.

Observing the people who pass in the street, Eliacim, with their hands in their pockets or a modest little package under their arm, a sadness usually comes over me which pains me, an anxiety which fills my conscience with vague remorse, which empties my eyes of charity.

I can't explain, my son, why the people who pass in the street have proper names and surnames inherited from their fathers, when it would have been much more human and more logical for them to go through life without a memory, or with the faucet of their memory blocked by a little glass ball.

The people who pass in the street, Eliacim, the sorrowful, numb people who pass in the street, my dear, with their malnutritions, their tubercular lesions, their frustrated loves, their never-fulfilled cravings, etc., walk along sowing stupidity and resignation over the evil-smelling little shops, and the calm brothels of the suburbs, a little bit with the unconfessed hope that death will catch them with their boots on, like the vagrant who made of his boot the tremulous flesh of his foot.

From behind the window shades of my window, my son, I see how the people who pass in the street walk, always listing a little, on their road to punishment. From my vantage point, Eliacim, almost all hopes are lost.

Chapter 198: The Sick People in Hospital

1.

How silently, how fearfully happy! Eliacim, the sick, the

men and women who are sleeping without documents, how happily! in the long and cold hospital ward, in the immense, wide world of the hospital, stealing from one another, and desiring for one another, wholeheartedly, death for one another!

How cautiously, how wisely poisonous, how tenaciously, Eliacim, the sick, the men and women who masturbate irresponsibly in the gloomy, humid hospital ward, in the enormous, out-of-orbit planet of the hospital, denounce one another with all their hearts, cursing one another to the grave!

How slyly, how hypocritically wicked, Eliacim, the sick, the men and women, who are dying without tears, how delicately, in the dark and dirty hospital ward, in the anonymous, miserable battlefield of the hospital, trick one another, offering, with their last ounce of strength, a kiss on the mouth to one another!

2.

Oh, my son! How fearfully, how wisely, how hypocritically, how silently, how cautiously, how slyly happy, and poisonous, and wicked, Eliacim, the sick, the men and women who sleep, and masturbate, and who are dying without tears, without responsibility, without documents, how tenaciously, how delicately, how happily, in the cold and humid, the dirty and long, the murky and dark hospital ward, in the anonymous and miserable battlefield, in the enormous, out-of-orbit planet, in the immense and wide world of the hospital, denouncing, and robbing, and tricking one another, and cursing with all their hearts, and desiring with all their hearts, and offering with their last ounce of strength, death, the grave, and a kiss on the mouth to one another.

Chapter 199: The Well-Matched Married Couple

The well-matched married couple I am referring to, Eliacim, are devoted enthusiastically to gossip. If the man next door has business which is not very clear, or the woman next door has a not entirely diaphanous love affair, my dear, the well-matched married couple to whom I am referring find out before anyone else, call a meeting, and publicize it. Didn't you know? Our neighbor, Mr. Raven's new Morris, according to what they've assured me, has come from the black market, surely, money cannot stay hidden! Or rather, didn't you know? the elegance, by all accounts improper for a girl from a middle-class family, of our little neighbor, Miss Agnes Whistle, don't you remember? yes, sir, that insignificant girl whom they call for in a car every afternoon, do you remember now? well, good, according to what they have sworn to me says nothing, but absolutely nothing! in favor of her virtue. Oh, my God, my God; this is what wars bring, my friend; depravity, and nothing but depravity!

I admire very sincerely the well-matched married couple I am referring to, my son, because they are people who have achieved a solid reputation in the entire neighborhood. Oh, Mr. and Mrs. Fishy! you can hear their victims say, a model gentleman, he; she, a bottomless well of virtues!

Chapter 200: The Chum with the Permanent Smile

With his little rabbit's face, Eliacim, the chum with the permanent smile lives on.

The chum with the permanent smile, my dear, is an amiable and obsequious little man who is really versatile, a Jack-of-all-trades. The chum with the permanent smile, my son, is one of the few remaining examples of his useful and convenient species, Eliacim, a species which is tending to disappear. (Therefore, when I see him, always with his permanent smile painted on his face, refusing to cease smiling, I favor him with my friendship and I bring him home to dinner once a week.)

The chum with the permanent smile, my son, is not English, but South African. The chum with the permanent smile, Eliacim, is from Ladybrand, in the Orange Free State, but he came to the Isles because of the war and he remained here, with his little rabbit's face, his reddish hair, his shining, gray, little eyes, his little musketeer's moustache, and his permanent smile.

During the war, my son, the chum with the permanent smile did not distinguish himself very much, that's true, and he was even censured on occasion by his superiors; but the fact is that war, Eliacim, you can tell by looking at him, is something which doesn't go with his feelings, something which clashes with his way of being.

I, my son, in spite of my dealing with him for some time now, don't know his name. Once I asked him, but he didn't reply in a very direct way, Eliacim, in any very clear way, Rolph, Osmond, John, Eddy. You can see that he prefers not to be called in any way, my son, but I am arranging things so as to come to an understanding with him.

One day I said to him: Would it bother you if I called you my chum with the permanent smile? and he replied, No, for Heaven's sake, ma'am! you flatter me! From then on, my son, I have always called him the chum with the permanent smile; it is somewhat long, but what can one do! that's his name.

(On only a few afternoons, Eliacim, when we prolong the

after-dinner hour, and we listen, with our hands intertwined, to "Good Night" on the gramophone which you gave me, do I dare to call him Chum all by itself. He, at those moments, usually kisses me without ceasing to smile. Later, pretending to have repented, he says: Can you give me a little marmalade? But I, my son, go along with his game and give him a little marmalade. What laughter! Finally, Eliacim, we kiss again. Chum, go! And Chum, walking backward so as not to turn his back on me, goes out into the street with the smile fixed, like a bird, on his little rabbit's face. I, from the window, usually wave goodbye. Goodbye, Chum! Goodbye, Chum! Goodbye, Chum!)

Chapter 201: Garden Statuary

Colder even than the gardens, Eliacim, the garden statuary, the Venuses which try to cover their breast with a finger, the Cupids with their quivers full of moss, the foolish Apollos, keep the secrets which are dangerous to reveal, secrets in which we all, they first of all, are implicated, secrets which would make us blush if they were known.

Within the cold heart of the garden statuary, my dear, the indigent frogs, the homeless frogs, sleep for the winter. A Czechoslovakian radiologist told me this one day, Eliacim, a really learned specialist in taking X-rays of statuary, my dear, the man who discovered that the Thinker, of Rodin, had a hole in his left hilum.

The fearful couples who try to make love in gardens, Eliacim, in the shadow of the garden statuary, tremble with dread when in the moments of silence they think about the lazy frogs which inhabit, in interuterine postures, the wombs of the primmest mythologies.

It is something which is very dangerous, my son, something which could bring about very disagreeable consequences, to admit, even though only in theory, that the garden statuary could run off at the mouth.

Colder even than the gardens, Eliacim, the garden statuary knows more about our affairs than is necessary. And the bad part of it will be the day they talk, the day their patience runs out.

It is something which the daring lovers who promise each other marriage in their shadow don't figure on. So much for them!

Chapter 202: Your Slippers

The other day, Eliacim, rummaging about in the bottom of a trunk, I found your winter slippers, your blue fur-lined slippers. Although the find, my dear, didn't please me at all, or almost not at all, I tried to overcome my feelings and I gave them to a poor man who comes to the house from time to time to beg alms. (I feel myself invaded by a rare calm which may be the forerunner of I don't know what.)

What I am telling you is that now nothing matters to me, Eliacim, nothing matters to me, absolutely nothing. The only thing I want is to get far away from me the slippers of the dead, my dear, the dead who don't need their slippers for anything; I want to put away from me the slippers of the dead, Eliacim, even though that dead man is you, who are dead, and more than dead, I know, dead with all your shipmates of the *Furious*, dead at the green and red sea-bottom, my dear; and you left your slippers, forgotten in your mother's house, at the bottom of a trunk, what sarcasm! without stopping to think of the harm you were doing, Eliacim, without stopping to think but about yourself, about your blue slippers.*

* Editor's note: Incomplete page (somewhat burned) in Mrs. Caldwell's original.

Chapter 203: Dawns

Yesterday I was ill, my dear, when I was writing you; I didn't have the strength to reach the bedroom, and I fell asleep in the armchair beside the fire. My letter of yesterday, I think, must have been burned. You have lost very little, Eliacim: I don't know what it dealt with, but most probably it was something inane and very far from you. What can we do about it, my son; one must take things as they come!

Well. When I awoke this morning dawn was breaking. A milky light began to appear over the houses while in the windows of the early risers there shone a yellowish and sickly light.

They are sad, my son, very sad, those dawns over the city, those moments when the old, thin city takes off her nightgown and shows us her flesh full of scars, her flesh furrowed by surgery like the bellies of unyielding mothers.

When you, still! used to come home every night, Eliacim, and you went to bed in your disordered student room, we didn't open the curtains until the morning had gotten up, until the morning had washed, and combed its hair, and primped like a bride, my dear, who awaits great and marvelous surprises.

But now, Eliacim, in this house everything is upset, because order is something which no longer interests anyone, something which we do not know, I don't know, my son, what to do with, and the curtains, some nights, even stay undrawn.

Through the window, my son, you can see the day which is being born without too much hope as if not to slight me. The first sounds of the city, Eliacim, the first steps, the first horns, the first whistles of the city, my son, still wail and sing, and cry out timidly, almost with respect, while the office workers, laborers, shop clerks, wash themselves like cats, put on their caps and their little scarves and go into the street, very much on guard lest they be scolded by the boss, or the foreman, or the master.

They are sad, Eliacim, very sad, those city dawns, those indecisive moments in which men still dare not speak out loud, and women, like vile beasts, urinate, unkempt and still half asleep.

Oh, my son, how sad are the dawns now for your mother, especially when she felt ill last night and didn't even have the strength to get to the bedroom!

(I'm somewhat better, Eliacim, thank you, and I am going to try to lie down.)

Chapter 204: What a Funny Dream!

I have just dreamed that you and I were getting married, Eliacim, to each other; what a funny dream! I was exceedingly nervous, Eliacim, and when the pastor asked you, Do you take this woman, etc.? I began to cry because I thought you were going to say no. But no, Eliacim, you did not say no; you are a gentleman and you were not going to lead your sweetheart to the altar and then tell her no; you looked at me, you smiled lovingly at me, and you said, in your firmest and roundest tone, yes, you took me for your wife. What hope it gave me, Eliacim, to hear you say it!

You were wearing a morning coat, with a nard in your lapel, and a pearl as big as a kidney-bean in your cravat, and I was dressed all in white, with a quivering bouquet of camellias at my breast. We made a very fine couple, Eliacim, I assure you, and the people watching us were touched.

Among my attendants were, what strange things we dream! your poor father (God rest his soul), and the chum with the permanent smile, a South African friend of mine about whom, perhaps, I shall speak to you someday. I did not even know the rest of my attendants or any of yours by sight.

To the strains of a wedding march which was composed just for us, Eliacim, you carried me in your arms out to the street. The guests asked you, Does she weigh a lot, does she weigh a lot? and you replied, No, she doesn't weigh anything at all, she's light as a feather, a real featherweight. Oh, Eliacim, what a funny dream, what a funny and happy dream!

The wedding reception couldn't have come off better; the guests ate, drank, and danced, and were happy and pleased.

When we were about to leave the hall, you put your arm around my shoulder, and said to all our guests: Gentlemen, I know that I am the envy of all of you; many thanks and good night. The guests laughed and raised their glasses to toast us: Long life, and many children! Oh, my son, how embarrassed I was!

On our wedding night I was very indiscreet and unoriginal, Eliacim; you need not repeat what I already know; but luckily, just when I was going to burst out crying, I had a fit of coughing which got me out of the difficulty, a coughing fit that made me laugh.

I sat up in bed, lit the light, drank some water, and kissed the photo of you which I have on my night table, a photo in which you are still in short pants. Poor boy!

Chapter 205: Healthy Reaction

There was a time in your short life, Eliacim, when you were very worried about healthy reactions, words which were your favorite commentary, almost your only commentary, on everything, or almost everything that happened. Had the cat delivered half a dozen sticky kittens covered with gray fuzz? Healthy reaction. Had the meter man explained the punch he gave, as a young man in 1925, to that Jamaican Negro who made a firecracker explode behind his back, in St. Leonard, beside the West India Docks, a punch which made the people shout exclamations of admiration? Healthy reaction. Had the neighbor across the way bought an electric refrigerator on hire-purchase? Healthy reaction.

It was a pleasure to hear you, Eliacim, all day long, handing out healthy reactions left and right, the same as a millionaire in healthy reactions who wanted to practice charity with the needy. What times, my son, what times!

I would now need very urgently, Eliacim, a healthy reaction, a violent and healthy reaction which would make me get out of the marasmus into which I am sinking, my dear, which would make me float, like a cork on water, above this boredom which dominates me, sometimes for hours and hours, fixed in my armchair, looking toward some corner of the ceiling, that corner which never opens nor will ever open to let a healthy reaction seep in.

But now no one repeats it to me, Eliacim; now nobody shows any interest that I may clutch at the last healthy reaction as if it were a straw.

I matter less and less, my dear.

Chapter 206: The Plaster Hand

If, at least, Eliacim, I had one of your hands in plaster of Paris! If only, my dear, I had one of your hands cast in plaster and cut off at the wrist!

Plaster hands, my dearest, are hands of the dead to a greater extent than the very hands of the dead themselves, Eliacim, and we mothers who would resign ourselves to keeping the ears of our dead son wrapped up in a linen handkerchief, how could we not give everything that was asked in exchange for one of our dead son's hands cast in plaster and cut off at the wrist?

I remember that when you wanted to make fun of anyone, Eliacim, you used to say, with the false gesture people usually use to tell the truth: He is such a ridiculous and grotesque individual that if he could, he would have in his house, cast in plaster and cut off at the wrist, the hand of the son he lost in the war; what a great bother.

Very well, Eliacim, that is my situation and you can believe me, my dear, that seen from within, this business of wanting a plaster cast, cut off at the wrist, of the hand of the one who was loved and is loved so much, and was lost forever, is something which is much less ridiculous and much less grotesque than you so riskily thought.

If I had your plaster hand with me, I would caress my cheek with it. I don't care at all what you may think. But, because I have to renounce everything, my son, I am to renounce even your coldest and deadest shape cast in plaster.

Although nothing matters to me, Eliacim, since I know that someday, perhaps the most unexpected day, you will return home like a little sea urchin, regretting so much useless navigation.

And that day, Eliacim, we'll set the bells ringing while people ask themselves, with their eyes wide open, what's happening?

(But only you and I will know this.)

Chapter 207: A Strange Visit

Today I received a strange visitor, Eliacim: a doctor with the face of a madman (I don't know who sent him to me), who spent two long hours asking me impertinent questions that I prefer not to repeat. What nerve, Eliacim; there were moments when I even laughed!

It seems to me, my son, though I don't know if I'm just imagining it, because at times I think they'll all end up driving me crazy; it seems to me, Eliacim, as I was saying, that customs are changing a lot, and that today doctors take certain liberties, above all certain liberties of expression, which they never would have dared to take before the war.

The strange doctor that visited me this morning, my dear (I don't know who sent him to me), spoke in a very low voice, in a voice that was almost impossible to hear, and I, Eliacim, since I couldn't get interested in his empty conversation, went on answering him question by question, yes or no, according to how I felt.

At times, however, you could see that he didn't like my answers, because if I said yes, for example, he would ask me, looking over the top of his glasses, Yes? Then I, as you will understand, said, No, no, I am mistaken, pardon me. Why should I contradict him?

The strange doctor, when I corrected myself, answered me almost ceremoniously: You are pardoned, madam. And he went on to the next question, to see if he would have any better luck.

My strange visitor this morning, Eliacim (I don't know who sent him to me), was not, even considering his excessive curiosity about the most intimate topics, how shall I tell you, overly out of bounds, nor, far from it, rude.

There's more: as he was leaving, he told me he found me very good-looking. No, I replied; I am no longer the woman I used to be; if you had seen me some years ago!

Chapter 208: Inventory

I've gone two days without writing you, Eliacim, forgive me. Maybe it's been more than two days; in any event, forgive me; I assure you that it wasn't my fault, my dearest.

I have been very busy preparing a minute inventory of the whole house: chairs, fourteen; armchairs, three; sofas, two, one covered in leather, and the other somewhat old, in garnet-colored silk that matches the curtain; tables, four; glasses, eleven, eight good ones, and three everyday, etc. This inventory business, my son, is a great burden, a monotonous, repetitive job: rugs, three, rugs for the side of the bed, four; beds, five; mirrors, five, two big ones, one of them broken, and three little ones, two of them broken, etc.

My best friends, Eliacim, you don't know them because they came after your desertion, are helping me with the inventory. They are very good, my dear, and they lend a hand; I think that if I were alone, and without anyone's help, I should have died of old age without seeing the end of my inventory. Our house is full of things, overflowing everywhere with things that kept piling up I don't know how; the strangest things in the world, Eliacim, the most difficult things to inventory: grandfather's death announcements, ninety-six; death announcements of your poor father (God rest his soul), three hundred (now I remember that I didn't send any of them out); death announcements of your grandmother, eleven, etc.

You know I always liked to have things orderly, Eliacim, and everything in its place; I demand, absolutely, that you believe me (kiss me); and the absence I am preparing for, my dear, an absence for the short while I need to restore my health, should leave me at peace with regard to the good order of our house.

The recovery of my health, so my best friends tell me, and I think they are right, requires the expedient of my taking a rest for a short period, as I think I've told you repeatedly.

I've gone for some time, Eliacim, feeling ill, with my spirits depressed (I have my reasons), my mood changeable (I have my reasons), and a difficult disposition (I have my reasons), which could not get interested in anything that was not you. I don't believe, God forbid, that it's really anything serious or of any importance (you know, my son, that I was always very strong), but my best friends—how they have cared for me! Eliacim, you have no idea!—recommended that I take a short period of rest, a short period of rest that may give me back my lost health, and my desire to keep on living, my dearest, to keep on loving you and remembering you every moment.

I have dared to pay attention to them, Eliacim, because it would be stupid to keep on being locked up between these four walls; understand that.

(Last night I dreamt I was entering a department store, an enormous department store, to buy myself a little boy doll. It was something I've needed for a long time, although the idea of going up to the toy department, to the doll counter, to say to the clerk: I want the most perfect doll possible, I don't care about the price, always shamed me, gave me an inexplicable shame. Then in the department store, I hesitated in deciding, because, the truth of it is that they did not have one doll that pleased me completely. After turning the store upside down, Eliacim, I chose one that looked like the clerk. This one, give me this one, please. The clerk looked at me, my son, standing under the light so that I could recognize him, and I couldn't keep from screaming. I fell to the floor; a crowd gathered and they brought me a glass of water. My son, my son, I have just seen my son, Eliacim! The clerk, elbowing his way through the crowd, fled to the street and went to hide himself in a brothel, under a bed that had a garnet-colored silk bedspread, like our curtain. I started losing more and more weight, my son, and I ended up being turned into an eyeless pigeon. I flew up to a roof, and there, at the foot of a chimney, I laid a little, round, rosy egg.)

Chapter 209: Goodbye Inhospitable, Filthy, Traitorous Home

Goodbye inhospitable, filthy, traitorous home! Goodbye cold, unpardonable walls, gallows wood, ferocious home! Goodbye foul air, foul memory, foul home! Goodbye Venetian blinds like dead eyelids, stairs that don't lead to happiness, merciless home! I have finished my inventory, thanks to the help lent me, of course, by my best friends; and I am going away without sorrow, even happily, and although I'm not saying it, without any intention of ever seeing you again.

I have erased all memory of you from our house, Eliacim, and if I had had the strength, my dearest, our house, right now, would be burning up in immense and trembling flames. But I didn't have the time, Eliacim, and, as I say, the strength.

Letters from the
Royal Insane Asylum

Chapter 210: Air

I have my room full of air, my love, a very strange purple-colored air that leads me not to think, that induces me to spend the whole day, lying helplessly on the bed, waiting for you.

I spent the night from dusk to dawn, my love, without sleeping a wink. This place is clean, strange, and cold; not cold in temperature, but cold in color.

(My best friends, my love, in spite of their promises, have not come to see me. Perhaps they haven't been able to come; perhaps all of their husbands suddenly died on them.)

I have my room full of air, my love. It seems to me that in this room there is too much air, my love, air under pressure, like in tires, air enough for breathing during all of a long life.

Chapter 211: Earth

In the earth in my room, my love, I have planted nard shoots, more than a thousand little nard stems, so that they can drink up the air, my love, all the extra air.

I have my room full of earth, my love, my body full of earth, my eyes, and my mouth, and my breasts uselessly full of earth, my love, a clammy whitish earth that is burying, poisoning my palate.

I didn't sleep last night either, my love, seeing how the earth grew, planting little nard stems in each new handful of earth that appeared, in each new handful of earth that fell from the mirror. (The first little nard stems that I planted, my love, kept getting lost under the earth that sprang forth later. But I am fascinated by the thought that this earth that advances and advances cruelly is ballasted with little nard stems, dead like children.)

In my room there is too much earth, my love. I would like to know that you are buried in my room, under the sink, among the nards. In the mornings, without anyone's seeing me, I would disinter you carefully, my love, so you could breathe.

And then when the earth filled all the room, we too would die, my love, embracing each other definitively.

It would be a graceful end, my love, an exemplary end, and one that my best friends (who still haven't come to see me) would envy with the most secret impulses of their hearts.

Chapter 212: Fire

I was not frightened at all, my love, to see my room full of fire, to see my room burning, to see my room overflowing with cautious flames that seared my flesh. I even came to feel, my love, a sweet and pleasant well-being, imagining—with what precision, with what diaphanous reality!—that you were laughing with a conscience as brittle as crystal, in the corner from which, crouching with your tail between your legs (a fleshy tail which ended in a fishhook of faded, clear green), you regarded the scene, happy to be before me once again.

Your bent horns were hot, my love, blazing perhaps from the heat, perhaps from remorse, and you watched me in an ecstatic trance, dressing and undressing, taking notes in a little notebook (something which annoyed me, relatively, for I am no longer the woman I was). To please you, love, I was dressing and undressing the whole day, at a giddy pace, and in a rhythm that tired me out and made me cough.

My room is full of fire, my love, and large burns rise on my flesh like big caressing hands, spread out like insatiable and wise hands.

But even though I know that the fire in my room is devastating and perverse, and of the same substance as the fire of hell, I feel very happy to know you are a witness of it, an exceptional and passionate witness of it.

(My best friends continue not coming to see me, my love; it gives me the impression that this must be at the end of the world, in some place which is dangerous to get to. It's not strange to me at all that they haven't dared to come, that they've been afraid to come.)

Chapter 213: Water

I can't cope with the water that falls from the roof, my love, that gushes from the walls, that springs up out of the floor, that spurts out of the furniture, and the bedclothes, and from the things I have arranged on my dressing table in a certain good order.

Water is something that grips me, something that drowns me, something I would like to keep away from me, my love, something that I would like also to have kept away from you while there was still time . . .*

*Editor's note: In Mrs. Caldwell's original, there follow two blurred, and completely undecipherable pages with obvious signs of moisture, showing unmistakable signs of having spent hours and hours under water, like a drowned sailor.

Afterword

Up to this point the pages that my unfortunate friend Mrs. Caldwell devoted to her beloved son Eliacim, tender as the maidenhair-fern leaf, who died heroically in the tempestuous waters of the Aegean Sea (Eastern Mediterranean), as perhaps the reader may already have had occasion to find out.

To our noble and mutual friend Sir David Laurel Desvergers, testamentary executor of the endearing old wanderer (whom I met in Pastrana stealing historic tiles and whom I always loved as much as respected), the quail-castrator and honorary member of the Royal Geographical Society of Gwynedd, I wish to express here all the unwavering gratitude he deserved for the confidence placed in me, confidence which I tried to reciprocate to the best of my ability.

Madrid, Spring of 1947—Los Cerrillos, Guadarrama
Mountains, Fall of 1952, with long interruptions.

Postscript

The Head, Geometry, and the Heart*

The head of a man is like a labyrinth of a thousand streams of water—torrential and wild at times; sluggish and slow and implacable at others; but it is never cautious and serene, flowing naturally with decent and sensible submission: never prudent, rhythmical, or civil. Man's head is very confused and bitter; it is full of mysterious keys and unknown echoes, and of registers of rhythmical or frantic sonority which is never fully understood: neither in peace nor in war, neither in orgasm nor in renunciation, neither in forgiveness nor in cautious betrayal. Man's head is not a trustworthy implement, nor is it a machine about which we know, with any certainty, what it is good for or is not good for: some use it for saluting respectfully; others, to lean it sweetly against the turgid breast of dying women; and still others—the more hot-tempered and passionate—for thinking up excuses and theories, syllogisms, hypotheses, and other frauds. Man's head is a corrupt pool in which man boils or ducks everything he sees or knows, everything he imagines, contrives, or

* Translator's note: This is a translation of the author's preface to the definitive Spanish edition of *Mrs. Caldwell Speaks to Her Son*, to appear in Volume VII of Cela's *Complete Works*, now being published in Barcelona. I wish to thank Professor Dalai Brenes for his assistance in translating this preface.

dreams. The sport of cutting off heads (now we know: like sugar cane, close and with one stroke) masks a prepoetic, not too mature, sanitary and moralizing subconscious.

Man's head may take three different forms: that of a cucumber, of a dodecahedron, and of an icosahedron. The first heads, the vegetable cucumbersome ones, are not pertinent to the immediate effects of what is being dealt with here; the second and third ones are. I will attempt to express my thinking about the numerals twelve, twenty, and thirty, not without first dusting off in my memory the line from the Book of Wisdom: timid are man's thoughts and uncertain their consequences.

The dodecahedron presents twelve faces; the icosahedron twelve vertices. The dodecahedron shows twenty vertices; the icosahedron twenty faces. The dodecahedron shows thirty edges, the icosahedron an equal number. The icosahedron is the conjugate polyhedron of the dodecahedron, since it may be obtained by joining the centers of its contiguous faces; the inverse is also true, because the phenomenon is reversible, and the dodecahedron, it therefore follows, is also the conjugate polyhedron of the icosahedron. Between Mrs. Caldwell, who died in the Royal Insane Asylum, in London, and her beloved son, Eliacim, who died in the tempestuous waters of the Aegean Sea, we are not interested —unless we wished to carry cruelty to its extreme—in the precise and final diagnosis of the regular convex polyhedron which corresponds to each of them. As a general rule (and since they are not figures which fit a man's head), it should be understood that three forms of regular convex polyhedra —the tetrahedron, the hexahedron, and the octahedron— shall be excluded, on principle, from our consideration; among the remaining ones—and in the specific example which concerns us—the particular assignment of a head to a form (or of a form to a head) of each of them isn't very important, since it's probable that, when each one of the forms relative to its contrary is a reciprocal conjugate polyhedron, Mrs. Caldwell and Eliacim will appear to us, indistinguishably and throughout their common lifedeath, their delightful and poisonous common death throe, to be in one situation or the other. Within the law of inheritance is nested the exceedingly complex egg of the fatal geometric nostalgia of biology, one of whose most beautiful principles teaches that the heads of a mother and son are reducible to conjugate formulae. The twelve (or a multiple of twelve) faces of Mrs. Caldwell can coincide, or not, with the twelve (or a multiple of twelve) vertices of Eliacim; the twenty (or a multiple of twenty) faces of Eliacim can coincide or not coincide, with the twenty (or a multiple of twenty) vertices of Mrs. Caldwell; nevertheless, the thirty (or a multiple of thirty) edges of the one are merged with the thirty (or a multiple of thirty) edges of the other, and we may assume that they are not different, but unique and common.

Chance is governed, as is biology, by the law of geometric nostalgia; the same is not true of codified (or at least established) law, which only attends to the surface of events—that minutia which history can record—and ignores the flying body—the essence of history itself. There are two pure or elemental forms (a premise which I must express so that what follows may be better understood) which circumstances may take, to wit: providence, or theoretical or probabilistic circumstance, and contingence, or pragmatic or positive circumstance. This contingent circumstance—in contrast to the most learned and providential circumstance—usually has nothing to do with spatial geometric representations, and, in consequence, disdains the correct harmony (which it doesn't believe in) of polyhedrism (which it doesn't believe in

197

either) and sacrifices, for the sake of the common good, so abused and always so much discussed, the principle of conjugate polyhedra. Well then: a specific contingent circumstance (I am alluding to censorship) castrated one face and five vertices of the polyhedron Mrs. Caldwell; observe that a pared-down dodecahedron or icosahedron ends up as pointless and eunuched as a sphere: in castrating—and, even less, in the vicious intention of the castrator—there is no middle ground, nor any halfway virtue, nor equanimity.

The face of the marriage and wedding night which an already ill Mrs. Caldwell dreamed was swept away, by the contingent circumstance which has been mentioned, at the same time as the vertices, which are now enumerated: the one about the eldest sons who masturbate at dawn, summoned by the hunting horn blown by the devil; the one about the hiding place of the onanistic children and of the materfamilias who prostitute themselves; the one about the woman who reaches the age for deceiving her husband (in Catholic countries this usually varies between thirty-five and forty); the one about the husband who reaches the point of being deceived by his wife (something which doesn't bother him in any substantive way); and the one about the irresponsible sick people who are given to the exceedingly sweet solitary vice. This multiple outrage which was committed against Euclid, not against the author of the book, blurred the precise outlines of both active polyhedra which, as a result, had to appear to us faultily drawn, or at least, not rigorously drawn. In the present edition the geometry is re-established.

My novel *Mrs. Caldwell Speaks to Her Son* is, in its apparent disorder, an act of homage to order, and in its illogical evolution, my avowed tribute to logical rigor. I shall try to explain myself. Pascal—and before him St. Augustine, and after him Max Scheler—knew what sorts of things the order of love and the order of the heart were. And Bergson, when he deciphers for us the essences of vital or desired order and inert or automatic order, instructs us on the evidence that disorder is but a mere practical idea, and of very limited range, since by it is usually understood, reducing by many degrees the desire for wisdom, all that which implies an unexpected order. Between public order—the pseudo-order of orderly people—and the extremely orderly chaos of the stars—which is rigorous, essential, and divine order: order at the edge of our resources—there is no more difference than that between misery and success or, said in another way, between the order of a Civil Guard and one of God.

This novel of mine was conceived, or intuited, as medicine for the spirit, although fundamentally not as close as might be supposed to the *Logique de Port-Royal* with Descartes as inspiration. I don't believe in the Wittgensteinian postulate that logic is no more than an empty tautology, but rather I think the tautology steadies logic with content (although it is clear not all logic may be reduced to tautology), and it steadies with sense the order which we still do not know how to define: Chapter 178, "The Iceberg," born out of the application of the formula for the permutations of four elements [factorial of four, $4! = 4 \cdot 3 \cdot 2 \cdot 1$], is a logical form which is judgmentally valid, which, checked in the tables, gives T [truth] as its result. Mrs. Caldwell was already mad when she wrote "The Iceberg," but madness embodies a logic as subtle as it is elusive, before which we must with humility confess our impotence. Paraphrasing John Dryden when he says: "There is a pleasure sure / In being mad, which none but madmen know" * (*The Spanish Fryar*, II, 1), we might agree that there is a logic in madness which only madmen know.

Shakespeare's lines, in *Hamlet*, with which by way of a

* In English in the original. Translator's note.

motto I begin my poem "María Sabina," are not far from this old way of feeling of mine: "Though this be madness, yet there is method in it." * Method, at the opposite pole from chance, assumes a road, it's true, but not which road it must be, and it is considered true that all roads—more or less directly and it matters little whether to the queen's throne or to a life of banditry—lead to Rome.

The schema proposed by John J. Doyle in his note, "The Hexagon of Relationships" (in *The Modern Schoolman*, XXIX, 93–94), could be applied to Mrs. Caldwell and to Eliacim, since their relations and interrelations (I have indicated in Iberic characters each one of the pertinent adjectivizations: equivalence [ᚼ], independence [ᛀ], contrariety [ᚴ], contradiction [ᚵ], subcontrariety [ᚻ], superimplication [ᚢ], and subimplication [ᚷ]) can be known and articulated. The hexagon would have the following form:

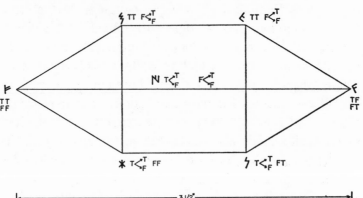

and (assuming a = first term, b = second term, T = true, and F = false) should be interpreted as follows:

1. *equivalence:*

$$a\,T \rightarrow b\,T$$
$$a\,F \rightarrow b\,F$$

* In English in the original. Translator's note.

Chap. 63: *The sundial doesn't run fast nor slow,* ⊬ no sundial is in error.

2. *independence:*

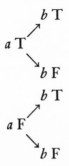

Chap. 41: *The dead are wont to assume surprising postures,* ⋈ all those who assume surprising postures are dead.

3. *contrariety:*

$$a\,T \to b\,F$$

Chap. 66: *The shipwrights sing beautiful sea songs,* ⊰ the shipwrights are mute.

4. *contradiction:*

$$a\,T \to b\,F$$
$$a\,F \to b\,T$$

Chap. 104: *The three daughters of Mrs. Sherwood got the measles,* ⊱ one, two, or three daughters of Mrs. Sherwood didn't get any disease at all.

5. *subcontrariety:*

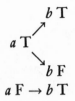

$$a\ F \rightarrow b\ T$$

Chap. 59: *The ogive arch is handy and genteel,* ↳ *the ogive arch is neither handy nor genteel.*

6. *superimplication:*

$$a\ T \rightarrow b\ T$$

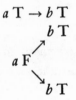

Chap. 47: *When I write these lines it is Monday,* ⚡ *I write on some Mondays.*

7. *subimplication:*

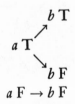

$$a\ F \rightarrow b\ F$$

Chap. 206 (in earlier editions, 205): *I know that some day you will return home,* ✳ *all prodigal sons return.*

In the preceding set of examples, I have copied from the novel only the first terms, which I have put in italics; the second ones are not certain, but they are possible in the castrating to which I was alluding earlier, of the regular convex polyhedron which might fit each one of the conjugate heads of Mrs. Caldwell and Eliacim. With it I propose to point out only the symptom of an attack against the most harmonious essence of geometry which, in the last analysis, is nothing but the indecipherable (perhaps it would be better to say: the still undeciphered) kernel of biology.

The outrage committed by the contingent circumstance of which, in its appropriate place, mention is made, has greater and more grievous effects, and in order to prove it, I would have had to have recourse to Hans Reichenbach's cube of opposition which, without complicating it, would have extended this proof more than was necessary. Nor is it too worth while to insist on the obvious.

This schema put forth in support of what we could call the geometric clarity of my pages (or, in a wider sense, of any other literary work: that geometry is an original and fertile science) would also lead us—it's not too far from this point now—to the polyhedric or multipolyhedric representation of my archetypes and even of the novel itself. The elements at work are 213 (as many as there are chapters in this unmutilated edition, since 14 bis and 60 bis, precisely because of their optional nature, don't count) and their correlation by vertices could be set up in an orbit of eight dodecahedra and seven icosahedra in alternate positions—and opening and closing the series with a dodecahedron—counting only the [214] empty vertices of the whole and considering unlinked (or linked to infinity) one last vertex, which I now call theological, and which represents Mrs. Caldwell's navel. The foregoing has been said so that a patient draughtsman can put it down in India ink, or so that Calder can give it its proper volumetric shape.

Mrs. Caldwell Speaks to Her Son was not understood very

well when it appeared, and I'm afraid that even today, except among readers with a very delicate seismograph in their consciences, it will still not be too much. I ought to add (by way of clarification) that I'm not surprised by the fortune which fell to my pages, which were probably written fifty years before their time; but I'm in no hurry—I never was—and I don't mind waiting, even beyond the grave.

Now, almost a quarter century after my encounter with Mrs. Caldwell in Pastrana, it no longer seems like a lack of charity—but rather like respect for the historical event—to state that around that time, my good and unfortunate friend was having an affair with the well-known guitarist Josué Jaraicejo Consuegra, alias Pifa, who gave her pleasure (and also beatings) and ran errands for her (and gave her Bujalance-style fritters). This Pifa, as is proper in a guitarist with self-esteem, was foul-smelling and harmonious, flamencoized and dogmatic, and although he was suffering from a hernia, he was also more patriotic than God (I'm using his own term of comparison). Mrs. Caldwell got a lot out of his company and enjoyed (in English and out loud, almost always reciting Coleridge's poetry) his Penibetic and dramatic acts of homage. Around that time, the techniques of tape recording were not yet very widespread in our country —a circumstance which deprives us of the possibility of leaving to the Museum of the Spoken Word even one trace of the intercourse between Mrs. Caldwell and Pifa—but, from the testimony of some listeners, the thing well might have gone, in certain circumstances, and more or less, like this:

Pifa: "Squeeze, you slut, or I'll punch you in the mouth!"

Mrs. Caldwell: "But oh! That deep romantic chasm which slanted / Down the green hill athwart a cedarn cover!" *

* In English in the original. Translator's note.

Pifa: "Shut up, shit, and move your ass the way you should!"

Mrs. Caldwell: "A savage place! As holy and enchanted / As e'er beneath a waning moon was haunted / By woman wailing for her demon-lover!" *

Etc.

Pifa and Mrs. Caldwell's affair lasted until the guitarist, who did things right, decided to substitute his love object, since she was already showing certain signs of wear, for the Hispanist Matthew G. Browning, alias Dante Gabriel Rossetti II, a colonel in the RAF reserves and a lyric poet whose muse was a flirt and full of feeling. Man's heart is full of mysterious and bitter crannies through which run, like a man in his own home, the two eternal fears: the fear of hunger and the fear of loneliness.

Pifa (we ought to finish off his sad story already) came to a bad end: the Hispanist, who was not very hygienic, but rather slovenly and gross, hit him with a brick as a sample of what was to come, and poor Pifa, anxious to cool off his twitching flesh in the clear water, dived into the Imperial Canal at the point where it passes through Garrapinillos and, we know that from his very reaction, he passed on to a better —even if more uncertain—life. His last words, according to the account of a young man who discovered him still breathing, were "Long live Spain!"

The heart of a man is like a labyrinth of a thousand streams of liquor: honey, bile, shit, and also blood which bubbles up out of the hole left by the knife. The drowned die with all their blood inside (those who drown in the Aegean Sea, those who drown in the Imperial Canal). And those who are hanged. And the strangled. And the poisoned. And the

---

* In English in the original. Translator's note.

starved. And the lunatics in the Royal Insane Asylum, in London, see how the water flows (this time cautious and serene, flowing naturally, prudently, rhythmically, civilly) from the ceiling, from the walls, the floor, the furniture, the bedclothes, the objects placed on the bureau, even with a certain attention to good order.